SPIRITUAL PATHWAYS

SPIRITUAL PATHWAYS

Paul E. Stiffler

To order additional copies of this book, contact:
Xlibris Corporation
1-888-795-4274
www.Xlibris.com
Orders@Xlibris.com
62052

CONTENTS

About the book

It did not start out this way . . . what began as a simple letter mailed to a few friends has now emerged to this book taking the form of practical, spiritual thoughts and actions which center around the seasons of the Church and calendar year.

Encouragement came like so many birds filling the sky while singing to lift the dawn; I saw a new day. Their music lifted my soul. Then came words of interest inquiring when this material would be published. This became the incentive for publication.

Years of celebration involving the seasons that touch our lives so deeply moved within me. The high seasons and holy days never failed to provide a deep inspiration in my soul. It is from these moments that I compose the words and images that are found in this book.

A pathway to spiritual growth is open to those who seek in quiet moments an awareness of the Divine. Here the mind will inform the heart and the heart will illuminate the mind forming a spiritual circle that gives balance to life. Each page invites you to enter an experience expressed in poetic form along with a guided imagery that can turn these quiet moments into a meaningful life experience.

This pathway reflects my personal journey of meditation which began in 1977 under the guidance of Sister Virginia Mary Barta of Marionjoy in Wheaton, Illinois and the urging of Rev. Dean Williams the Chaplain as well as my wife Elsie and family who have watched and encouraged the recording of my spiritual journey This is my effort to share with many what I experience. Join with me as we follow these pathways.

About the author

Paul E. Stiffler, D.Min.
Minister of Pastoral Care, Western Springs, Illinois
Ordained 56 years; married 59 years

Title: *Spiritual Pathways*

Years of Pastoral duty and Theological thought brought me to where I am today. In 1951, as a student in seminary, I was assigned to the First Evangelical United Brethren Church in Downers Grove, Illinois and continued there for four years. I then moved to Faith United Church of Christ on the South side of Chicago serving as both an associate and senior minister until 1963. The next seven years were given to First Congregational United Church of Christ in Kakankee, Illinois. My next full time pastorate for 24 years was at Community Congregational Church (United Church of Christ) of Villa Park, Illinois from where I retired in 1994.

While in Villa Park both my spiritual and theological journey culminated by receiving a Doctor of Ministry degree from Bethany Theological Seminary in Oak Brook, Illinois, however studies in spirituality still continue. While in retirement I served First Congregational Church of Dwight, Illinois, part time at Peace Memorial Church in Palos Park, Illinois, and presently part time Minister of Pastoral Care at First Congregational Church in Western Springs, Illinois.

Looking back to 1994 at which time Elsie and I moved to our home south of Kankakee where the Iroquois and Kankakee Rivers conjoin. A friend, Dan Jones, his brother Paul, Elsie and I built a 16' X 20' studio which we named *The Centering Place*. It was in this studio that I began to write materials which carries that name following the Church and calendar year. Poems centering on the liturgical seasons and guided images were written as one might write while on a spiritual journey. I now share these personal reflections of more than 56 years as we venture together on this spiritual journey.

Dedication

I dedicate this book to my wife, Elsie, and my family
and those who encouraged me along the way
as well as those who find
The Centering Place
truly a spiritual path to follow.

About Liturgical Seasons

Advent

Advent begins the Church year consisting of four Sundays leading to the celebration of the birth of Jesus. Previously, Advent was considered to be the same as the season of Lent lasting as long as seven weeks. Around the 11th Century, the reign of Gregory the VII, it was changed to four weeks.

Christmas

Christ's Mass was discovered to be celebrated in Spain about the year 325 C.E. Most of the Christian world celebrates December 25th as the accepted day. Though widely taken as a correct date, some thought as in Orthodox belief, places January 6th as the proper time of Jesus' birth which coincides with the coming of the Wise Men. Shepherds "in the fields watching over their flock by night" was a ritual occurring in the Spring. (Any attempt to make a correct date will have to be approved by the children of the world).

Lent

Lent, a period of forty days excluding Sundays, refers to Jesus' experience of being tempted by his refusal to yield to the temptor, and at the end was healed by the Angels sent by God.. Lent begins with Ash Wednesday at which time the mark of the cross is made from the ashes of the previous year's palms waved on Palm Sunday while Jesus made his entrance into Jerusalem. Holy Week closes Lent with Good Friday, the day of crucifixion.

Easter

Easter, the first and foremost celebration of the Christian calendar, centers around the resurrection of Christ. The Gospels record this major event in sightly different ways, each one leading to the discovery of the empty tomb and Christ's resurrection. Because of calendar difference Orthodox Christians celebrate a week later. Easter is the first Sunday after the first full moon after the Vernal Equinox. There is a close connection with the Passover which accounts for different dates. Easter is the first and foremost of all celebrations. All other calendar days swing around this one single event.

Pentecost

Fifty days after Easter, according to the book of Acts, the followers of Jesus were assembled in one place on the day of Pentecost, a celebration of the Feast of Weeks. Their excitement over Jesus rising and appearing among them caused accusations of being drunk which Peter refutes. Written in an imaginative way, the wind rushes upon them at which time several languages were spoken all of which each one understood the other. The intensity was likened to flames dancing on their heads.

Advent 1

As Advent begins the liturgical year for Christians, so may reading this book begin a new journey for you.

An element of quiet prayer is expectation. Quiet prayer allows for the soul to look beyond every day concerns while still 'leaning' toward the world from which the soul has come for its re-creating moment.

For all the biblical announcements about Messiah—and I love their beauty and hope—it was not the dramatic earth shaking event which fulfilled expectation. Rather, in solitude and aloneness heaven's gift was given and hope slid down the rays of a celestial constellation. "How silently, how silently, the wondrous gift is giv'n. For God imparts to human hearts, the blessings of his heav'n." So Phillips Brooks writes of it.

Advent holds up the expectation of the heart in its quiet stillness when God steps into our lives. Living with expectation is part of our spirituality. Advent is a season in which the soul can prosper.

Expect God's gift. Even in my dark moments there is always a flicker of expectation. I have found difficult times easier to endure when I allow expectations to come out of the wings and take center stage with all the other player-moods in my life. This does not brush off serious contention. It adds divine dimensions to sorrow, regret and grief. "Surely God will guide me into healing and hope" is a prayer of expectation.

*   *   *

Why do you persist in satin luxury
when straw will do?
Cows and sheep are my royal guests,
shadows offer enough space for my light.
I will come there—
in greying barn lumber
splintered by ages
yet enough to cradle
My Love.

Advent, 1994

Images for your quiet place

In this season of rush and tension, be sure to find quiet places for yourself. Even if it is a moment or two, that is enough. Even if it is stepping into a doorway and relaxing for a minute that is enough. Recall passages or images that will refresh your spirit. Following is a meditation you may use for this Advent season.

1. Find a space that you call your own. It is vacant now and empty. It is your space where you imagine a building taking place.

2. Build a stable where animals can find shelter and warmth.

3. Arriving builders follow your instructions. Watch as they begin to work. The foundation is carefully measured. It is exact and will be sturdy and warm.

4. Completing the foundation, now the exterior walls are constructed. Again careful measurements are taken. The timbers are cut to size; inside supports for the roof are placed.

5. Crossing from one side to another, the beams become part of the roof. Strength is necessary for the roof to hold its covering. The upright timbers are ready for the roof.

6. Completing the outside of the building, the interior is given attention. The timbers are used to divide the room. Stalls are formed. Eating and watering troughs are in place. Mangers are ready where bales of straw and hay provide a place to sit.

7. Look at your stable; all seems to be ready.

8. Draw close to what you have created. As best you can become part of it; let your spirit become ready.

9. Open your stable place. Once vacant now this special place stands in expectation.

10. Invite creatures of the earth to take their place. Let them join with you by adding their soft noises. Let a prayer rise to God: "I am waiting now. I am ready."

11. Become aware of a distant light moving toward the stable.. It stops overhead. Beams push through the roof covering playing all around you. It touches dark corners. A new light has come.

12. Dwell in these moments. Let come what may. If you wish to share this with someone ask them to be with you. Alone or together simply wait. As one thing after another comes to you, look at them until you find something of meaning.

---

13. Linger with what has been given to you. Enjoy and celebrate God's gift of peace and goodwill to all. Pray your gratitude.

14. Ponder what has taken place. Return to your daily life with the energy of service to God and humanity.

15. Go with a mission of Hope.

Advent 2

What ancient cry ever rose so high
   to Holy Listening
   inarticulate yet understood
   given voice beyond speech?

What heart beat ever rose to flow in tandem
   with Sacred Harmony
   undefined and deepest need—unknown
   even in the breast where it took residence?

Were You always coming from first beginnings
   Thou Advent of greater Love
   in celestial announcements we did not see
   written long before life took shape or form?

Is there a child of surprise that never goes away
   coming, ever coming—time and place
   by Thy Holy Knowing
   entering winter doldrums of the soul?

What primal cry of mine did You hear
   did You know in ancient grottos of my heart
   where you were coming, ever coming
   invading my darkness Thou Holy Light?

What song ever declared wondrous Love and Hope
   Thou Holy Tenderness
   making whole my fragmented way
   coming, ever coming—undeserved Grace?

                                     Advent 1997

Images for your quiet place

Expectation is the inheritance of rich Hebrew tradition. Advent, a late addition to the liturgical year, affirms that which has long been part of the soul's journey into higher consciousness—Yahweh hears the cries of humanity. That is true today as ever. Ardent desires converge this year as the holy days of Hanukkah and the eve of Christmas merge. Prayers, like the Shofar, call attention to the One who is present in all ages to all people. No special language is asked for when praying; human needs are already known and gifts prescribed. Following are prayers for each Sunday of Advent (1997) based on the lectionary readings for that day:

Advent 1
Jeremiah 33: 14-16; Luke 21: 25-36

Thou Lord of Righteousness, all that is around us withers, being a parched and desolate people wanting for justice. In the midst of shriveled hopes, Your promises are sure. We give thanks for the certainty given to our living. You made known to us, in prophets of old and in Jesus of Nazareth, Your compassionate compact to save. It is in that Infinite keeping that we have our safety. Hear this prayer of gratitude for all those times in which Your pledge of coming has been fulfilled; we name them before You. In the name of Messiah we honor You as we have been honored. So be it!

Advent 2
Malachi 3: 1-4; Luke 1: 69-79

Thou God of Tender Mercy and Righteousness, Your gentle whisper breaks into the constant commotion of clamoring voices; it is Your word that rests our souls. Keep us alert to messengers coming our way. Refine and purify our coming and going that Your Holy Name would be honored. Oaths of mercy have come true. We have been touched by Infinite caring and we name those moments now . . . So be it!

Advent 3
Isaiah 12: 2-6; Luke 3: 7-18

Thou Holy One of Israel, Strength and Might, we trust You and are not afraid. Our thirst for salvation is assuaged in the deep well of Loving Mercy. You came to us to winnow all unholiness; Your anger becomes comfort to us. We are baptized into new life by Your messengers hand of Love. These moments we offer and name them now . . . So be it!

Advent 4
Micah 2: 2-5a; Luke 1: 39—55

Holy One of Peace, it is our hearts which leap for joy. Majesty and honor are Your due. Create within us a birthing of joyous Love as You did so long ago. It is too much at times for so great a Love to be given to us. We have longed for it and in its presence are startled as Holy Goodness leaps beyond our imagined hopes. We are touched by magnificence and now sing its song as we offer those moments . . . So be it!

Advent 3

How do I know of such comings?
  Is it heart-dancing that tells of unfolding advents?
  or song leaping and bounding from hill and tree?
  can it be celestial illumines staggering
    imaginations, interrupting routine cadence?
What of dawn cracking open darknesses
  or brightest star lingering, pointing to story,
  or fluttering wings spreading messages of
    divine import?
How do I know of such comings?
  do they impinge their advent deep within
  when crying provokes the heavens?
  or pleading child-faces lifting to skies above?
  or dusty strangers seeking shelter
    for birthing hope?
What of ancient planets meeting in convention?
  or sky observers finding breakthroughs
    in zodiac formations?
  or searching Word and land for advents yet to be?
How do I know of such comings?
  is it slamming doorways that awaken advents
  or nestling hay welcoming flesh-tone evidence
    of Love?
  or soft and gentle nursing life toward chance?
  or streets filled with milling humans wandering and
    wondering of mystical events startling
  or simple wonder, wandering?
How do I know of such comings?
  of advents?
What of searching sky swooping within and
    making room in
    manger places I did not know of before?
How do I know of wonder, how do I know of miracle?
How do I know the Advent of Love?

         Advent 1998

Images for your quiet place

Commercialism is often seen as an intrusion into religious and sacred celebrations such as Christmas and Hanukkah. Think of these as the Divine intruding into the mundane, into the worldly, into the profane. Advent reverses our thinking. Let all that is in our celebrations find a new expression, one that is profound enough to startle, to tremble before majestic songs and words of "Fear not!" Let Advent invade the season and reclaim dimensions of the Holy.

One way of doing this is to choose a symbol for the Holy day being celebrated such as a Christmas tree. You may have others that you favor. This example forms a pattern that you can follow:

1. After quieting yourself, visualize a forest filled with rich greenery. There are many different kinds of trees. Snowy landscapes could be part of your inner picture.

2. Look for a special tree among the many before you. Choose one and stay with your choice.

3. Find a comfortable place to sit. Simply gaze at your tree. The surrounding sky is a quiet blue, almost like velvet. Let this be your special tree.

4. Place familiar ornaments wherever you wish. Some of these may be from your earliest recollection, childhood, or special occasions. Take your time in doing so. Look at them carefully recalling your fond memories.

5. Begin to create symbolic ornaments from your experiences such as birth, Baptism, Confirmation, Marriage, a moment of awakening or conversion, special and private times which changed your life. Create a form which symbolizes each special event. Slowly and lovingly place them as ornaments on this tree.

6. Continue to gaze at this decorated tree. Add ornaments that are part of your celebrative story. Begin with the young maiden who hears the angel message. You may wish to shape Mary's Magnificat into an ornament. The kindly, older man, Joseph can be placed there along with the donkey and other traveling needs. The silhouette of a city may come to mind.

7. Notice that other ornaments may appear by themselves. If that happens, allow for it to continue. They may have a special message to you. Keep placing your own along side them.

8. Move toward the top of the tree placing an angel who calls out, "Fear not!" Simply look at the figure and listen to the words.

9. Notice that all around this chosen tree the sky has become a deeper blue, so blue and calm that many sparkling stars can be seen. They form a background for an angel chorus which sings out: "Glory to God in the Highest, and on earth Peace to all."

10. Stay with this meditation for a while, then let it go returning to your daily life making note of how much the story of celebration is part of your own story. Rejoice and be glad for it.

Advent 4

How can I expect you to come
when all I have is this crowded stable
filled with animals that supply heat
provide food and become my barter
my sole possessions and security?

How do I expect you to come
when all I have is a manger for you to lie in
a bale of hay where you can be birthed
splintered boards for roof and side
which are not enough to keep out cold?

How do I expect you to come
while all around beggars push through streets
guards swagger with swords
widows and orphans cry out for help
and prisoners weep for mercy?

How do I expect you to come
while hope hangs as a silent harp on willows
heart songs no longer echo in the hills
peace is captive waiting for ransom
dreams and prayers have faded way?

How do I expect you to come
into this unsure heart of mine
dreaming as if a fantasy would be heard
making ready my lowly station
still looking for stars to guide?

How do I expect you to come
in silence which is mine to give
in secret whispers of Almighty Love
in adoring maiden willingness
in my quiet waiting for a miracle!

Advent, 1999

Images for your quiet place

We are in the midst of the Advent-Christmas-Epiphany cycle which moves through a season of expectancy to the birth story to the manifestation of the light and power of Christ. God's solidarity with humanity is realized. One of the original special days, Epiphany, was the third chief event in the Christian calendar of the early Church.

Wise Men coming with gifts is the portrayal of this special day. Today, women, men and children bring gifts for the baby in a manger.

In a reflection of our own lives, having seen the star and tried to follow it, begin with the earliest celebration you can remember. Let it contain all that you can recall. Toys, visits from relatives and friends, Christmas caroling, tree trimming, favorite stories being read all make up pleasant and warm scenes.

Continue on through your life. Observe the changes at various stages of your living. Also, observe how you changed and what these festivals now mean to you. They may have become brighter, or in some cases filled with shadows. Keep moving on and let the remembered years speak. Continue this way until coming down to the day in which this image is taking place.

As the festivals continue, prepare yourself to make the journey along with the Magi and others. Distances other than geographical ones may need to be covered. Spiritual distances can be overcome now; drawing closer to God as you did as a child.

Bring a gift to present either at the manger or directly to Jesus who rises from the baptismal waters or walks among the guests at the wedding of Cana.

Look into yourself; inspect the endowments which God has provided in your life. What is it that you choose to bring? You are offering a gift of yourself before a great and majestic moment when earth was affirmed by God again saying of life, "It is good."

With this gift there is opportunity for what you bring to express love toward humanity. How will this take place? Visualize a way to make real what you bring for God honors those who do so.

Let this be a time to which you return. Keeping your heart and mind open, listen for the guidance of the Holy Spirit. There is no longer separation. In its place there is a Presence for which the soul seeks.

Advent 5

Shuttering and chilled the earth awoke
To find its bleak and barren way
A silent land where no one spoke
Of whom this darkness would but stay.

How could we know Your heart was leaning
With untold love as ne'er before?
Your eye with watchful care designing
For Grace had heard the soul's implore.

Heavy the sighing hearts so keening
And earth with cosmic chills composed
A saddened song of lone despairing
Of brittle broken souls disposed.

How could we know Your heart was leaning
With untold love as ne'er before?
Mid groans of creaking earth so pleading
Angelic wings began to soar.

And spread across the sky with glory
Some piercing light began to shine
A cosmic smile with radiant story
All harbored ills with joy refine.

How could we know Your heart was leaning?
With untold love as ne'er before?
Thus into dark came One redeeming
For us the swaddling clothes he wore.

How can we know Your heart is leaning
With untold love as ne'er before?
In humble simple ways of cradling
Now comes the Holy Visitor.
Advent 2000

Images for your quiet place

In olden times the people of Israel anticipated the Messiah. Knowing the presence of Jesus called Messiah, how can we achieve this same experience of high expectation during the season of Advent? Read again passages from Isaiah chapters 9, 11, and 40. Include any others which you select. With the above setting as an atmosphere for quiet prayer, you may follow these ways, one step flowing or melding into another. Experience a recycling or a spiral of each movement, (i.e. from receiving and reflecting to a period of quietness then opening, finding a gift, reflecting on it until returning to daily activities.)

1. Quieting. Let all of the noisy distraction be subdued in as much as possible. (Recognize built in sounds such a creaks in your home, furnace fans, a chiming clock.) Embrace as much quiet as possible.

2. Waiting. Here you do not need to develop a plan, agenda, or assemble a schedule. Allow yourself to wait even though you may feel the bumps and nudges of the mind to "do something" which is an ordinary and a daily inclination.

3. Opening. With some freedom from our own agenda, let there be a flow of divine offerings, like a stream that bubbles with fresh oxygen. When a celestial present compels the soul to give attention, open yourself and let it come within.

4. Receiving. This lovely gift, which comes from the heart of God to your own, appears quietly, silently, and asks to stay with you. Give it birth.

5. Reflecting. Ponder the wonder of this divine generosity. Rather than fitting this benefit into a plan of your own, consider how your life will be nourished because of this blessing of "manna in the wilderness" from which all before us have partaken.

6. Praying. A wonderful conversation takes place in which the heart gives praise and thanksgiving for the closer relationship with God and a sacred connection with the Universe of which we are a part.

7. Returning. There may have been one or more spirals for you until, finally, a sense of returning presents itself. Having received and prayed, changed and lifted, daily life beckons and coming back is with a new step.

.

Advent 6

O my soul
Make angels in the snow
Leave imprints of Divine attention
For our lives are bleak with woe
On layered cold from heaven's sky
Make angels in the snow
Sweep arms and legs in circles wide
Cover lands with heart's tradition
Pattern the earth on every side
Make angels in the snow
Appear once more and sing again
And tell of peace, goodwill
Remember songs with sweet refrain
Make angels in the snow
Bring magic to the souls of men
Courage to right our wrong
Let one brave act of hope portend
Make angels in the snow
For God, to us His Grace will lend
Invite a child to make it so
For they with joy and love pretend
Make angels in the snow.

Advent, 2003

Images for your quiet place

It was in an occupied land where the angels sang their song of hope. Hearing angels in a noisy world is the work of our soul. It was quiet on the hills of Bethlehem except for the sheep and shepherds awaiting lambs. It cannot be said that it was silent, but the contrast of angels bursting into the birthing atmosphere with words and song must have been startling.

How can we hear angels in a noisy world amid the rat-tat-tat of gunfire, cascading bombs hitting the ground with loud impact, or the crying out of innocent victims? Angels are present in occupied lands now as then when shepherds were watching over their flock by night. Let this quiet time be a prayer for angel songs to crescendo beyond the noise hovering above homes and within hearts.

1. Create the image of war-torn deserts: dry, dust filled air, smoke from artillery, craters and skeleton-like buildings and homes.

2. Soldiers and civilians are going about their daily tasks creating a life they must live. Children seek places for a safe playground.

3. Let expectations of God's advent rise as a stream of shining particles moving upward, spreading in every direction as if the sky were a basin for collecting a common cry for hope and peace.

4. Allow for the angels' song to become distinct, clearer than any of the surrounding noises.

5. Now, everything and everyone stands still for a moment. There is a fallout of peace and goodwill. Hear it again singing in your heart.

6. Prayers take shape within each person. Each glance, each look, becomes the prayer for healing. All forms of separation fade replaced by a sense of being one family.

7. Noises that were pervasive, with their constant insistence for our attention, lose their power as the advent of God's message takes a new hold over the earth. Thank God for this gift.

Advent 7

O the journey!
Long and tiring.
Stones bruising
stumbling, wounded feet,
thirst grasping the throat
and all to find a birthing place.
How terrible the heat of desert,
the unending doubt,
restless wondering,
the long fatiguing trail
laying down its own conditions.
Sparse is the name of this pilgrimage.
Scant and lonely
this inner duty which comes in the night;
an angel voice telling a naive heart
not to be afraid;
fears refusing to be subdued.
Who would choose such a way
this way of ways?
Who is it; who?
Why, could it be you
whose throat is parched,
whose soul is hungry,
whose feet are bruised?
Your pilgrimage, your journey
that seeks a birthing place;
for angels tell of it
commanding attention
and so travel this earthen path
with its many arrivals;
it's Bethlehem waiting.

Advent 2006

Images for your quiet place

These twelve-word free verse poems give a picture of Advent. Each one moves closer to Jesus' birth. Use them in the weeks that follow as a focus for your prayers. If you write your own verse allow for an image or subject to present itself as you pray and then be guided in using whatever words come to you.

First Sunday of Advent
Watchmen
tell us
of
midnight caravans
seeking wonder
in
desolate
warring lands.
Second Sunday of Advent
Inns
close doors
as
love seeks
in
open hearts
a
manger space.
Third Sunday of Advent
Star
amid stars
beckons
my journey
to
birthing love
which comes
again.

Fourth Sunday of Advent
Light
drawing near
with
Love's intensity
makes
His room
within
my heart. .

Advent 8

Love falls silently
as a first snow,
with her gentle embrace,
covering bleak landscapes
and lo,
all seeing,
all hearing,
is transformed.
Long suspended dreams come true,
waiting rewarded,
coming with Love you always knew.
Advent stars crowd skies
once dreary
with unrelinquishing sadness;
souls downtrodden,
weary
from wornout prayers.
Empty hillsides, eager for songs,
find melodies
written on snow heaped staffs;
wood railings, dotted with bird notes,
link fenceposts on countrysides;
streams, bubbling with happiness
on some merry, winter journey,
slice through drab waterways;
unexpected dramas tingle souls.
God's Love; ever coming, is coming,
is coming, is coming, is coming, is here!

Advent, 2008

Images for your quiet place

Sacred celebrations such as Christmas and Hanukkah turn our minds and hearts to the Divine; the Divine intruding into the mundane, into the worldly, into the profane. Advent gives us a chance to make our celebrations find a new expression, one that is profound enough to startle, to tremble before majestic songs and words of "Fear not!"

1. Visualize your town or neighborhood. Walk through a section of the city near you. Take in the brilliant lights, the decorations, the small scenes of the manger.

2. Look for special accents and creative displays. Imagine the mind and heart that brought that scene into being..

3. Stay in front of each one for a moment. Linger as long as you wish.

4. See what are familiar ornaments depicting some aspect of the story you know from your earliest recollection, childhood, or special occasions. Take your time in doing so. There is no need to hurry. Look at them carefully and let your memory be touched.

5. Imagine members of this household coming out with bundles of decorations, laying them down, planning where they are to be placed.

6. Gaze at the activities taking place. Then, in the corner of your eye, watch for the invisible presence of the Shepherds, some Bethlehem towns people all crowding around the developing arrangement.

7. Step into this imagined scene. Sense the expectation and joyfulness.

8. Enjoy the fun of a child-like imagination. Feel the exhileration. which was present at the manger so long ago.

9. Carry the hope and joy of Christmas as you continue your walk. The creative heart of God has stirred the neighborhood and us with it.

10. Return to your place in life and bring with it the merry celebrations for which the heart longs. Create peace and goodwill wherever you are able.

Christmas 1

Nations rage but seldom totter
        darkness seems the only light
One more voice to raise its cry
        out of earth's infested blight.
Where is it that our eyes can look
        darkness seems the only light
Where blacker holes of galaxies reign
        what sign will set the heart aright?
Look to edges of the universe
        darkness seems the only light
Born in distance yet born each time
        stars assembled incarnate bright.
Vault of heaven where planets play
        darkness seems the only light
Light years stretching surround Bethl'm town
        outer space has sets it sight.
Edge of town and edge of life
        darkness seems the only light
Streaming doorways beam the way
        daytime in the midst of night.
Boundaries of a pit-black sky
        darkness seems the only light
Manger crib and brightest skies
        God's gift of Grace and Might.
                Christmas, 1997

Images for your quiet place

Rich images fill the combined holy days of Hanukkah and Christmas Eve. Hanukkah in the Hebrew means "dedication". The Maccabees had won religious freedom and rededicated the temple in Jerusalem. The miracle is in the burning of candles for eight days when there was fuel for only one day. As each day passes, the "helper" candle, used for lighting, ignites one, then two, then three candles until all are lit. At this time gifts are shared. Christmas Eve presents God's gift in Jesus, first as a baby and then the man of the cross and resurrection. Gifts are exchanged at Christmas time with lighted candles and festive worship picturing the stable scene.

These two festivals are here for us. Let your spirit choose an image related to one of them. Now quiet yourself to be led in the direction you need to go. If using the Menorah, watch for the brightening of its glow. Take the "helper" candle to the first candle and let its glow brighten. There may be light shed on a blessing, a need, a relationship clarified, or choosing to live your life in some new way.

Over a space of time which you can determine, continue to light the candles; first one, then, the next time two, then three and so on. Each candle could mean something different to you. Take what is there and go with it. As each of the lighted candles bring more illumination, so its revelation develops. Faith increases, closeness to God is made stronger, and dedication has a more firm hold as disclosures of new life are offered. The Power of God is present and close to you. Enjoy, for it is yours. Soft burning candles recall Holy faithfulness and provide a warm hearted setting into which revelation may come.

The doorway of the stable in which Christ was born fills the street with its streaming light. Gradually, as the doorway opens, more and more light streams forth. Stand at the door ready to open it slowly. Recall the power and drama of that moment. As is true with the Menorah candles, it is better to become accustomed to the brilliance than to suddenly be flooded with such mystery. There is no hurry for the days of celebration are many (8 days for Hanukkah and 12 days for Christmastide ending with Epiphany).

The stable light may touch your own life, or someone you love, or about whom you care. Watch as its healing encloses a special person in its warmth, touching deeply both the body and the soul. Let it stay as long as you can and then let it go. (If it is too intense stop your meditation and go back to the stable door once again.) May the festive lights brighten your heart and home.

Christmas, 1997

Christmas 2

Angel-speaking electrifies
this star filled night
touching darkness that is my own
tending as usual to routines
fear and trembling are in charge
replacing faith with fright
     Rising from ancient earth vibrations
     shaking energies send their ohmmm
     while heavenly messengers
     shower blessing in cavernous shadow
     hidden even to myself
     and peaceful song in soul's catacomb
Two angels came with gentle sooth
o'er pain and trouble spreading wing
Tianna sang and Aspen too
a sweetness that only God knew
"there is peace for your shaking heart"
of such good news did both sing
     "Fear not" their echo never fading
     "we bring you more to see
     than ever seen before
     more than life surrounding
     celestial gifts all bearing
     God's kindness called heart-free"
"We come," called Aspen and Tianna,
"with good news in our birthing
look closely for God revealing
is with us in myriad secrets
let earthly treasures take their place
we come with joy assuring"
     Two angels flew into night
     and changed it into morn
     "Fear not" with Son of God combined
     "good tidings of great joy"
     beyond all thought perceiving
     Love within each soul now born
                Christmas, 1998

(Written for two young children who were very ill)

Images for your quiet place

Planetariums provide the much needed view of star filled nights. Our city lights invade that special territory and we cannot see as the ancients saw a canopy of a captivating creation. Even so such a spectacular sight is available to us through the gift of imagination. This is one way of adding peace and calm to the rush that still lingers.

1. Provide a starry night for yourself. You may have such a view in your own backyard. If not, remember a trip to a Planetarium, or a picture you have seen, or develop a scene of the heavenly wonder that dwells in your mind and heart.

2. Take time in doing so. God was not rushed, so you need not be either. Let the creating of many stars take time. This is useful as a relaxing method and for providing a way into quiet meditations.

3. Watch for "falling stars" as you meditate, gazing at them as they disappear. This too, can bring to you both quiet and peacefulness. It may also serve as a way of freeing yourself from troubles, by attaching them to a star and letting them fade from view.

4. Look for Zodiac formations as the stars assemble. If you know enough about them, their pictures may inform you of something special; a message just for you.

5. Single out a star and continue to look at it. It may be that a star picks you! Either way this star holds a gift for you.

6. Ask "what message do you have for me?" When you "hear" something accept it graciously without comment or thought. Go on by asking the same question, "what message do you have for me?"

7. Discover that all the "expected, traditional" thoughts soon leave and you are given newer considerations, some that are hidden behind what is always in your thinking.

8. Accept whatever happens even if it has come to you before. It may be that these important thoughts need to be assembled in your heart once again. God knows what to give us in these moments of praying.

9. Anticipate the appearance of a new Christmas announcement. It could be folded into the familiar birth stories for there is much in each one that deserves our pondering as did Mary, the mother of Jesus.

10. Stay with it as long as you wish. When you finish linger a while longer. What am I to do now? The Shepherds asked that question. How does this message bring good news to my life and others? Where is the peace and goodwill that I may bring in the name of Love?

Christmas, 1998

Christmas 3

Gentle the noise of cattle lowing
Quiet the sound of Shepherds kneeling
Soft the sound of Mother nursing
Sweet the sound of infant breathing.

So this is how You chose to come to us, thou Holy Power, who could sweep us away. So this is how You chose to come to us by placing Baby Jesus in a manger's hay.

Swift the Love that God is sending
Bright the radiance now descending
Peaceful the Angels' song now singing
Calm the earth in silence resting.

So this is how You chose to announce to us, Thou Holy Wind of Heaven, who could blow us away. So this is how You chose to announce to us the coming of Your new day.

Dark the sky with stars now glistening
Silent the hillside, Ewe's now birthing
Darker still the world now praying
Bending close, your Love now listening.

So this is how you chose the day for us, Thou Holy wisdom from on High, who could have looked to another world. So this is how You chose the day for us by touching our lives with Your Grace unfurled.

Hear the Christmas prayer now praying
Hear the dreams for peaceful living
Hear the heart which most needs healing
Hear the children who most need feeding.

Infant Child who hears their pleading
Bethlehem Babe whose heart is heeding
Enter our hearts a manger making
Fill us with Christmas in our homeward leaving.

Christmas, 1999

Images for your quiet place

We are in the midst of the Advent-Christmas-Epiphany cycle which moves through a season of expectancy to the birth story to the manifestation of the light and power of Christ. God's solidarity with humanity is realized. One of the original special days, Epiphany, was the third chief event in the Christian calendar of the early Church. Wise Men coming with gifts is the portrayal of this special day. Today, women, men and children bring gifts for the baby in a manger.

In a reflection of our own lives, having seen the star and tried to follow it, begin with the earliest celebration you can remember. Let it contain all that you can recall. Toys, visits from relatives and friends, Christmas caroling, tree trimming, favorite stories being read all make up pleasant and warm scenes.

Continue on through your life. Observe the changes at various stages of your living. Also, observe how you changed and what these festivals mean to you. They may have become brighter, or in some cases filled with shadows. Keep moving on and remember the day in which this image took place.

As the festivals continue, prepare yourself to make the journey along with the Magi and countless others. Distances other than geographical ones may need to be covered. Spiritual distances can be overcome drawing closer to God as you did as a child. Bring a gift to present either at the manger or directly to Jesus who rises from the baptismal waters or walks among the guests at the wedding of Cana.

Look into yourself; inspect the endowments which God has provided in your life. What is it that you choose to bring? You are offering a gift of yourself before a great and majestic moment when earth was affirmed by God again saying of life, "It is good." With this gift there is opportunity for what you bring to express love toward humanity. How will this take place? Visualize a way to make real what you bring.

Let this be a time to which you return. Keeping your heart and mind open, listen for the guidance of the Holy Spirit. There is no longer separation. In its place there is a Presence for which the soul seeks.

Christmas, 1999

Christmas 4

Thou,

       Selfless Giver of our love
       Wondrous Splendor of our heart
       Tell what giving I can bring
       As Yours which came from up above
            Only that my soul would sing
            And joy to everyone impart.

Thou,

       Spirit on the wings of fire
       Burn through the mists of our decay
       Crumble carries of hatred
       Saddened souls with hope inspire
            O Love all wrapped in manger bed
            Giving resurrection day.

Thou,

       Passion bound to us earth
       Filling shadows with your light
       Gracing life, most tender, kind
       Bring us to our second birth
            Our souls which you forever bind
            Peace and goodwill both shining bright.
                     Christmas, 2000

Images for your quiet place

Firm evidence was found that Christmas, or Christ's Mass, was practiced in Rome in the early fourth century. In the year 274, the emperor Aurelian had introduced on December 25 to the imperial city a festival of the Invincible Sun, (Natalis Solis Invicti). So some time before 336 the church had begun the celebration of the incarnation, the birth of the Son of Righteousness. Some scholars think of this as the beginning of the liturgical year. Christmas is one of the most widely observed of all Christian feasts. Here is found a way to find light in the midst of winter gloom as well as our response to the message of "God with us", Emmanuel. A brief formula for finding light in our darkness rests on being still and using our imagination.

1. Sit in stillness and let your eyes wander through the sky. If it is cloudy you can still "see" them (stars) in your memory. You may even see a "shooting" star and trace its trail across the heavens.

2. Create this starry image from an experience before hand, or from a trip to watch a planetarium perform its wonder. The Christmas Star program creates the time and the exact arrangement of the stars as seen at Christ's birth. Use a chart to help you.

3. Continue to watch upward or inward as you begin to feel that you are a part of the heavens and the heavens a part of you. You become one with the celestial vault.

4. Feel the darkness which is softer than imagined, not cold or sterile. Rather sense its presence as being warm with life in it.

5. Be open to revelations here. Humans have observed the cosmic arch since time began. Both guidance and hope have been discovered.

6. Picture what the angelic chorus was like at the birth place of Christ with its shimmering background, and songs pouring forth. (If you use music this may enhance the experience.)

7. Open yourself for the message which angels bring. It is for you. Let the soft darkness hold a new light for your soul. God touches you and speaks to you. No matter what has taken place, this too, has been part of life events. Carry the light coming into darkness as God's gift and then celebrate with all your heart.

Christmas 5

Write songs on my heart Angels of God
As you did when Christ was born
Scratch deeply new melodies
Across world darkness
On mountain tops
Let it blaze
In valleys below
Let it fire the color of peace
In rocket's glare
Ride the course of rivers
Streak deserts with rainbow blossoms
Turn oceans upside down
Plunge into their surface depths
Swimming in darkest blue
Stay mysterious for the sake of awe
Pipe for my child to dance with glee
Play instruments no one can play
Strum strings of harmony
Drench the Universe with sweetness
Let not my vision close to wide-eyed wonders
My soul shrink from startling bliss
My ear deaf to humming wings of love
Come, oh come, Angels of story and myth
With your Truth
Create life in my straw-strewn heart
From which all who feast
Are nourished with love
Peace and Godwill
I am in need of divine merry
Interrupt with late-breaking news
Of Hope.

Christmas, 2002

Images for your quiet place

Nestled in the darkness of the city, a small beam of light lines the street with its stripe of welcoming warmth. There is something unusual taking place, not just then but now as well for the city is ours. The transport of choice in these reckless days is with the heart, the inner eye taking in all views from high places and low. Its attraction is the longed-for rescue from misery and sorrow brought on by our own ways. Page after page in the scriptures are devoted to the deepest desire of the soul to be at peace with God and thus at peace with one another.

There is a way to follow, a daring way, which asks as much of us as it asked of God. The streaming light must go from the center of our being with peace and goodwill toward everyone. God sent the Son, not to patch up our blunders, but to be the light upon a new way. An old longing is met with the consistent answering of the Divine whose light seeks to penetrate the smugness of doing things in our own way. Combining the will of our mind with the will of God blends the necessities for world peace. Spend a moment of quiet in this manner as you open yourself to the light that moves aside all darkness. Follow in this manner:

1. Quiet yourself and let your heart move familiar scenes of Christmas across the screen of your thought.

2. Choose one scene which may picture your favorite nativity describing the event of long ago.

3. Stay with your choice as you gaze at this familiar scene. Find the opening, a door or a window or a slight crack in a wall where light finds a path from its confines and spreads out into the surrounding area.

4. Let that light shine slowly and easily while embracing you and all that it touches. The light is warm and gentle and does not seek to commandeer your life. Observe that it blends with the light within you. Watch as two sources come together as one.

5. Look steadily at this new blend. You may find this to be a calming of anxiety. Peacefulness comes forward.

6. Let this light shine into the world you know along with many different nations and faiths illumined by its widening scope. Let it continue to shine upon all with its peace and love. The gift of God's peaceful light comes through you.

7. Let these images go but know that this light will forever shine within you on every street you walk. Here is Christmas itself.

Christmas, 2002

Christmas 6

Christmas Proclamation

Hear Ye, Hear Ye, Christmas is here!
Seek ye out that barren place
where God's great love is born.
Hear tidings which the angels bear
one early Christmas morn.

Hear all who listen with your heart!
Look for light where darkness reigned
where God's great love is born.
Hear the braying, praying heart
one early Christmas morn.

Hear the murmuring doves above!
Bend your heart to what they say
where God's great love is born.
Hear sweet Mary softly sing
one early Christmas morn.

Hear rushing shepherds drawing close!
Listen as excitement dawns
where God's great love is born.
Hear them whisper all that's told
one early Christmas morn.

Hear once more the angel's singing!
See them in your manger heart
where God's great love is born.
Hear the glorious praise of heav'n
one early Christmas morn.

Christmas 2005

Images for your quiet place

Through the centuries the road to Bethlehem has been well traveled. It is a road that you may have walked yourself listening to Scripture, observing a church Christmas pageant, or sitting quietly while your imagination roams. Using this gift can bring a calm spirit moving into restful moments of healing. The Christmas Gospels bring a variety of images which lead to manger places that heal and restore with the wonderful promises that God has made and which are constantly delivered. Follow this guide as you give time to consider the birth of Jesus.

1. Find a comfortable, quiet, warm place where you can let your imagination roam.

2. Picture the road to Bethlehem. You might use a Christmas card, or a map of the Judean countryside, or go back to a time when you visited the holy land and placed your feet on Bethlehem's streets.

3. Start your walk from wherever you choose. Perhaps it is on the outskirts along the Jordan River, or even in Nazareth where Mary and Joseph began their journey to Bethlehem.

4. Walk this pilgrimage alone or with someone you choose as a companion. Perhaps others will join you as you welcome them to walk beside you.

5. Engage in a quiet time going over the story of Christ's birth and, on occasion, telling your walking companions something that is taking place in your heart. Share the story of your good news with them.

6. Approach the manger however you might imagine it. As light glows from within each of you are drawn toward its healing power. There illness of body and soul is met with love and mercy.

7. Kneel before the manger symbol of God's love. Let the light pour over you making you whole. With angels say, "Glory to God in the highest heaven, and on earth peace, goodwill among all peoples." Return in peace.

Christmas, 2005

Christmas 7

Bethlehem, Bethlehem,
        little House of Bread,
Did you know that Light would shine
        from your midst,
invading a world of dread with hope
        once lost from view,
that in the smallest feeding trough,
        splintered and rough,
would come, as it was said,
        a ruler who is to shepherd my people
        Israel?
Did you know that wisemen led
        by stars, traveling from afar,
paid homage in a back yard barn
        to innocent Love swaddled,
that shepherds rushed to see and tell,
        sped by angel songs,
to kneel with the smell of heated animals
        bunched in a stable
watching a baby now abed?
        Did you know, Bethlehem,
that heaven burst with glorious song
        as earth, subdued, shifted
while few took note
        as God slipped into our world,
that, little House of Bread,
        we would by grace and love be fed?
Did you know, Bethlehem, Bethlehem,
        that we were born there too?
        Christmas, 2006

Images for your quiet place

Shepherds, startled by the angels, caught their balance upon hearing the words to not fear. Announcing the birth in Bethlehem the heavenly host proclaimed that the child would be found wrapped in swaddling cloths and lying in a manger. The story tells how they "made haste" in seeking the chid who was born. Take this time to join them as you picture yourself being part of their excitement in going to Bethlehem.

1. Travel with the Shepherds down the hillside that lead to Bethlehem. The hills have many rocks and stone as you follow a winding path.

2. Watch carefully as the town begins to emerge from the darkness. Few lights are available. Stars do their best to illuminate the path.

3. Stepping into the gate at the city wall the many directions that the streets offer becomes visible. Choose one of them knowing it will lead you where you want to go.

4. Looking around you darkened homes and houses offer little light in your searching.

5. Turning a corner light, coming from the stable of the inn, floods the street. It becomes obvious that this is the place of which the angels spoke. With the shepherds you move quickly and see that everything is as it was told with Mary, and Joseph sitting quietly and the baby Jesus lying in the manger. All are in awe.

6. Knowing that the lambs are birthing in the hills the Shepherds turn to leave and you stay alone in the stable as the darkness now comes and the scene in you heart fades.

7. Breathing deeply you say a prayer of thankfulness knowing how you have been touch by this event in which God showed his love for the world. Be in harmony and peace toward all with whom you share life.

Christmas 8

In one small corner of Planet Earth
a carpenter bends o'er splintered wood,
ordered at someone's behest,
choosing as is his daily chore
wood that is the best.

A small order, unimportant
perhaps, as such request will go,
but still, his self now put to test
will try and do his very best.
He, though rough hewn
as wood in his calloused hands,
considered his project, loved it,
though it was so very small.

Who knows the hungers it will feed,
this tiny, insignificant manger,
stuffed with fodder, hay, and seed,
or what its tiny frame will hold
when winter comes: frigid,
lonely, bold.

His was not the only eye
his labor to behold
for God had found this special craft,
from very far away, and said,
"Here is where I birth my Love,"
and chose that splintered bed.
Where honest souls and roughened hands
seek to do their part.
God places there His greatest gift
and comes in a humble heart.

Christmas. 2008

Images for your quiet place

1. Find your way to the manger.
2. Imagine what it was like in the mid-thirteenth century when St. Francis placed the first living nativity for all to see and know the story of Christ's birth due to the fact that most people could not read.
3. Begin wherever you are or choose to be, outside Bethlehem where the sheep are birthing lambs, one among many visitors who have come to pay their taxes, or from some special place in your life experience.
4. Approach the town and walk down its streets lit only by the lights of night.
5. Following a bend in the road there is a light thrown across the street from an open door. It has a different glow to it—strong and steady, intense, yet comforting.
6. Move slowly, easily toward that lighted area. Take your time, no rush is necessary.
7. Moving on, you may experience a calming. As you close the distance the light draws you to itself. It is secure and safe.
8. See the entrance to a stable, a cave used for animals and livestock.
9. Looking into the small, rather chilly quarters the source of light can be seen in the midst of a gathered family.
10. Feel the warmth from the animals while observing the loving concern of Mary and Joseph.
11. Serving as a manger, a small feeding tough illuminates the stall now shared with living things surrounding a hallowed place.
12. Stay there for a while—as long as you wish. Enjoy the scene in any way that you choose. Stand back and simply watch, or enter with others and become part of the activity. Whatever you want to do is what needs to be done.
13. Leave sensing differences in your thinking or feeling—your walk, your intentions, your being.
14. May this Christmas experience bring you peace.

Christmas 2008

Lent 1

Prayer of a Penitent
You have asked that those who have eyes should see
       and all I did was merely look not seeing
You have asked that those who have ears should hear
       and all I did was merely abide the noise
I did not see You in a child's tear-stained face nor
       Your smile across the wrinkled face of age
       nor did I see Your brokenness in the bending body
       of frail handicaps
for all I did was look.

I did not hear the sobbing of a mother's tortured sadness
       as when You cried over the city
       nor did I hear the pity of Your great heart in vacant
       and wandering exiles
for all I did was tolerate the noise.

Is there a time that I have sobbed and You did not listen
       or was so empty of body and spirit that
       Your pity did not come
       or wander in self-imposed exile and
       You did not recognize the sigh of my soul?

Is there a time that as a child I was hungry and
       You did not feed me the bread of life
       or in aging my spirit wrinkled with time
       You did not restore my soul
       or felt brokenness of body that I could barely move
       and You did not rush to make me whole?

I have received while withholding Grace and still
       abundance is showering upon me
       goodness and mercy following me
       peace and goodwill in ample supply

What is it I can become when my heart is heavy
    my spirit shadowed with the past
    my mind cluttered with remorse
Am I still Yours, Thou Creator of Love?
Lent, 1999

Images for your quiet place

"For he will command his angels concerning you to guard you in all your ways. In their hands they will bear you up, so that you will not dash your foot against a stone" (Ps. 91:11,12).

With the millenium-speak that is going on as well as the crashing-computer-crisis one would think these are the only words addressing the coming Y2K event. Quieting the self and reaching back to ancient words remind us of unchanging truth, constant and comforting. It is there for us all the time, a source of confidence as we continue with living. As a way of resting in this thought, follow these steps:

1. Relax sitting in silence for a few moments before beginning the next step.

2. Be aware of the deep snow (1999) that covered the Midwest. A gentle thaw followed which helped to recover the grasses buried by the storm.. Other areas had fog or cloudiness which changed the landscape. Simply watch the deep snow that covered the Midwest as it thaws as it thaws revealing of ground cover and grasses.

3. Visualize this revelation with patience, awe, and expectation. Hidden and yet evident, this transformation points to an eternal care. We do not see how it works but we see what comes of it. Soon, changes are everywhere.

4. Watching over you God provides the gentle and necessary transformation of the earth which are His messengers, symbolized as angels.

5. Affirm this, "I am in God's keeping" for surely you are. It is a promise revealed long ago upon which a life-time guarantee was founded. God's angels carry his command to watch over you. Enjoy such presences in your life.

6. Continue your meditation until you are ready to let it go. You will know when that is. Go about your life peacefully for you are in God's keeping.

" . . . the angel of the Lord said unto them, 'fear not' . . . ."

Lent 2

What is a heart but Sanctuary?

Come I bid you
  wandering seeking souls
  my heart is a Sanctuary
  for Holy Love therein abides

Come wounded for I am wounded too
  all who suffer sadness and remorse
  with blazing scars and doubt
  soothing balm waits for you

Come all who have been thrown away
  who are rejected and despised
  for I was discarded too
  embracing love circles round

Come all who live in darkness
  cast away from all light
  for I was entombed as you
  light will always find its way

Come I bid you
  in your seeking wandering way
  my heart is a Sanctuary
  for Holy Love therein abides

What is a heart but Sanctuary?
        Lent, 2000

Images for your quiet place

Among the many prayers which Richard Foster lists in his book *Prayer*, is Examen of Consciousness. This prayer is one of introspection, of examination, of seeing how God has been present for us through each day. Examen stems from the Latin and is the name of the indicator on a balance scale, and thus, becomes "an accurate assessment of the true situation" as Foster writes.

Lent may become a special time for a period of introspection (examen) and appreciation for your awareness of God's presence each day. Follow these steps:

1. Begin each morning with a greeting. Let there be a thank you to God for restful sleep for the body and merciful kindness for the soul.

2. Review the landscape that is to become day for you. What is waiting to be done, to address, to care for, to cure? Look from a high point which includes as much of the total day as possible.

3. Sing a song of Presence or hum a familiar faith hymn so that there is melody in your heart. Perhaps a tune comes to you, one not heard before; a melody that God is composing.

4. Spiral down in your flight to a particular aspect of your day. Remember that you are taking many gifts with you; especially this: you are not alone.

5. Assess what you will do with your choice as it connects with the pleasure of God. Let the song burst forth once again.

6. Begin in whatever way wisdom points. Since love casts out fear approach your duty, job, privilege, or stewardship with a compassionate caring. Be filled with joy.

7. Return to where you began the morning and in retrospect look at the day once more, reflecting on how God has been with you, on how earth activities open the way to heaven's work, of how balance for heart and mind and soul was taking place. And be glad for it, saying a prayer of thankfulness to close the day. And may you be open to those surprises which nurture and sustain.

Lent 3

No wilderness matches boundaries
Of mercy
Nor barrenness
Where temptation wiles seduce
You have lodged Your Presence
Within my very soul
As snowdrifts gathering
Surround vulnerable shoots
Sheltering promises lying in wait
For Spring resurrection
Silent and soft
Descending as snowflakes
In a streetlight glowing
Spirals embracing lunar legs
Moonbeams from heaven caressing
Earth's luxurious bosom
In assorted patterns
Cooling balm in heated fervor
Proposing powers without limit
To earnest hearts
Open
Resonating with ancient truth
Word and bread interchanging
Abating hungers
Angel hospitality sustaining
Visions of divine influence
Enticing spirit's prowess
Exciting body and soul
Lovers
In hollows of hallowed Hand
Woven
Entwined.

Lent, 2002

Images for your quiet place

On any athletic field, court or track, what really shows up is preparation. It is true also of any endeavor in life. Any given moment which is either offered or thrust upon us will expose the length to which we have gone in making ready for challenge, accomplishment, or strengthening of body and soul.

Easter was almost a season from the very beginning. The forty hours of Friday to Sunday were increased finally to forty days, excluding Sundays which are always considered feast days. The preparations are longer than the event to which they guide us.

Time reserved for a special work is a most important feature as we move through our life. To travel toward a special ceremony, such as Easter, takes the same time whether you provide a concentrated effort or not. Why not shift priorities to refresh the soul? Lent is an appropriate season for doing so. (Keep a journal of reflection, something that records the markers of your own path.)

1). Purchase a journal book that has a good binding. Spend a little more for one that has gold like edges. Give importance to your writing. In using a loose leaf folder the sheets separate and become lost. A bound book will keep your pages together as well as helping resist the temptation to throw away a part you may find uncomfortable.

2). Choose a Scripture. It may be a parable, the Sermon on the Mount, a letter, a narrative. Page through the Bible Topical Index for subjects that are appealing to you.

3). Plan to read this chosen portion of the Word through the entire season. Stay with your selection and allow it to open your mind and then your soul.

4). Record the day, the time, the year in which you write. This is important as you look back, perhaps over several years. It is a history of your spiritual travels.

5). Just write. Let yourself be guided as though your pen is being moved by a force within. Let it rest after you finish. It is not necessary for you to analyze your work. Leaving it retains an initial response. At the end of this secured period read your spiritual travelogue and write what you have found.

6). Move into prayer. It may be silent or thankfulness for what has taken place.

7). Now action takes place. Without referring to your writing ask: "What shall I make of this day?" "How will I become aware of God in everything I do?"

Lent 4

What was it like for you out there
With wilderness heat pressing in
Withered trees with branches bare
What was it like in that desert din
With mountains reaching in the air
Layers of sand swirling and thin
What was it like Oh Jesus fair
Did hunger ready your soul to sin
Did dry parched lips speak despair
How did those 40 days within
Alert your heart of tempter's snare
Waiting to give your soul chagrin
Or sharpened mind become aware

"Stones to bread is quite a spin
Plunge from towers just a dare
To get it all you just begin
King of the world so debonair
It's quite powerful and masculine
Be easy and devil-may-care
Just be sincere and genuine"

With God's Word none will compare
Angels in deserts abide therein
Abating soul's deeper starving glare
Beyond temptation lies your origin
God's healing power your soul repair
For angels are you next of kin.

Lent, 2004

Images for your quiet place

The wilderness and the solitary place shall be glad for them; and the desert shall rejoice and blossom as the rose (Isaiah 35:1).

Great promise is listed in this chapter: weak become strong, blind eyes are opened, deaf ears are enabled to hear, waters breaks out as streams in the desert, and a highway appears called "The way of holiness" (vs 8).

Luke 4 records that "Jesus being full of the Holy Ghost returned from Jordan, and was led by the Spirit into the wilderness . . ." (vs 1). At the end of the temptations, Luke writes, "And Jesus returned in the power of Spirit into Galilee . . ." (vs. 14).

The wilderness, whether it is a place into which you can go or a life situation in which you feel alone, know that the Spirit goes with you, and when all is said a done, returns you with power. This meditation may help you in this season of Lent:

1). Enter into a quiet time. You may imagine it as a desert or wilderness. Create a separation from all things that surround you.

2). Remain quiet for a moment. Let this be a time when you are not asked to put your mind to work.

3). Open your senses to a spirit that is with you. You need not do anything except allowing yourself to be in the presence of being accepted.

4). Watch as the flow of inspired awareness seems to answer questions in your life.

5). Give yourself over to being completely guided through these under girding moments of clarity.

6). Settle quietly into the one moment that seems like home to you. Stay there and be led by an illumination other than your own thinking.

7). Return to the place which life has for you, going forth in the power of the Holy Spirit into all that is now clear. Be glad for the revelation God has provided.

Lent 5

Lifetimes abound with wilderness
and desert sands
    with few tiny blossoms in barrenness
    sun burning and dry
    thistles and brambles scratching deeply
    beyond skin and bones and flesh
Some wounds
    more easily healed
    place bodies on alert
    and as intended assert
    the way back to being whole
But what of soul
    of my soul I ask
    through trudging years—40 I would guess
      or 40 days for that
Of what purpose this journey
With illusions of magic bread
    or flying through the air with some
    curious chance of landing safe
    or of kingdoms come
If only there was a magic way
To water and feed with incredible power
Then I could get through
    this lonely desert/wilderness
If only I could live such dreams
    at least in these 40 Lenten days
Then maybe
    just maybe
Angels would heal my soul.

                        Lent, 2005

Images for your quiet place

Tsunami horror, fresh in mind and heart through video coverage, gathers our world in common heartfelt charity. (2005) Humanity rests on these moments of personal and national response. Prayer vigils are made in every country and religion. Our prayers include victims, survivors, families, and those holding on to hope. Mudslides and avalanches alike have cast their lengthy shadow upon the nation bringing them closer to home than ever before. We know not what to ask, but we keep in prayer those caught in these catastrophic events. Meditate in this way:

1). Sit in a comfortable and quiet position away from noise and intrusion. Let peace descend upon you.

2). Prepare to replay some of the jarring and repeated scenes you have viewed. Be as observant as possible while saying prayers of blessing on all you see.

3). Begin to let the pictures of these tense and dramatic moments flow past you in a continuous pattern.

4). Include the many smiling faces of children now back in school and survivors as well who battled the intensity of the rushing waves. As these scenes come and go, let them find balance between what you first saw and what you now view.

5). Observe what is most often repeated in your mind's eye. Let something in particular come from out of this general viewing and keep it in focus.

6). Give attention to this particular visual that reoccurs and continue your offering the love, blessing and hope which comes from your heart. As it becomes your prayer, feel it radiate across the miles to the person or situation that has presented itself. Stay with this prayer.

7). Draw your meditation to a close, and as you do be open to a way of supporting the hope and the love that you see is possible. Let God bless you and direct your calling.

Lent 6

When Spirit nudges you into wilderness
go without fearing what is yet to be,
taking with you an open heart,
a hungry soul.
Above all be ready for a journey
that takes longer than you think.
Pray to find how full its emptiness.
Do not fear howling winds at night
filled with a desert mirage
of empire building,
or paying no heed to nature's law,
or manufacturing bread out of rocks
for stones remain stones
except when they shout praise as Jesus passes by.

Don't be in a hurry for time to pass.
Each moment bulges with secret revelation.
Gather myrrh from trees and shrubs,
and frankincense as aromatic prayer;
add golden surrender to a Love larger than yourself,
and pray for it to never end,
for wilderness empties you into the world
that you never left.
See at this portal footprints of another day
with designs in sand by angel wings
healing the Healer whose shadow now falls upon you.

Lent, 2006

Images for your quiet place

In a recent Kemper Letter, Bob Kemper gave sound direction for being in the midst of trying situations which exert negative powers. He suggest using a mantra which has power to offset strenuous circumstances and lift you above it and into another dimension. One source of mantra phrases, which are worth repeating, comes out of the scriptures. It is here that the soul is informed. You may recall this passage from Isaiah: For your thoughts are not my thoughts, nor are your ways my ways, says the Lord. For as the heavens are higher than the earth, so are my ways higher than your ways, and my thoughts than your thoughts (55: 8,9). Continuing with Bob's direction, Images presents a few passages from which you can choose a single word, a phrase, or a special thought that presents itself. Keeping the phrase short avoids stumbling over too many words. Instead of the entire passage, find a word like "rest" or "redeemed" or choose a phrase within the text such as "God heals the broken hearted," or "You are mine."

As you read the following, think of them as whispers from the scriptures:
1. Be still and know that I am God (Psalm 46: 10).

2. In returning and rest you shall be saved; in quietness and trust shall be your strength (Isaiah 30:15).

3. Let not your heart be troubled, neither let it be afraid (John 14:1).

4. God heals the broken hearted, and binds up their wounds (Psalm 147:3).

5. Come to me all you that are weary and are carrying heavy burdens, and I will give you rest (Matthew 11: 28).

6. Do not fear, for I have redeemed you. I have called you by name. You are mine. When you pass through the water, I will be with you; and through the rivers. They shall not overwhelm you. When you walk through fire you shall not be burned, and the flame shall not consume you (Isaiah 43: 1,2).

7. I have cared for you from the time you were born. I am your God and will take care of you until you are old and your hair is gray. I made you and I will care for you. (Isaiah 46: 3b, 4).

Ponder these words. Read them all at once or separately. In repeating them over and over, you will discover a gift of renewed strength and hope.

Lent 7

Heartprints,
unlike footprints in the snow,
are not easily tracked
as in the wildness of desert
where sands shift and cover over
where you have been
or where you intend to go.
Drifting snow hides as well
leaving obscure patterns,
suggesting a presence
whether aimless or not,
in the midst of its drift,
a sometime playful,
sometime determined
presence.
Heartprints reveal soul
with its etchings
scratched deeply from beginnings,
far and away from things mortal,
where divine intersections
declare journeys yet to be made.
Winds of the Spirit blow
and rearrange destinies
that the heartprint gives
tracking its design to love deeply
and forever.
Be unafraid my heart,
continue on for in wildness
winds uncover your prints
for things holy are in waiting.

Lent, 2007

Images for your quiet place

Jesus constantly returned to a familiar place of prayer finding a fresh sense of God's guidance and love. Are your favorite places always the same as if frozen right where they were the last time visited? Is there a shift in the landscape with natural or manmade changes? Perhaps inner changes occurred which makes your special site different. Changes hold within them a freshness that touches the heart, mind and soul.

Lent comes again and ends with the new dynamic of present time and new personal experiences. Prayer awakens your needs, hopes and dreams. As Lent brings you to your chosen place of prayer, follow these suggestions:

1. Choose a place to pray by using a picture of Gethsemane from a book, or one that you have imagined. (You may create your own garden as a place to spend a quiet time.)

2. Stand before this picture and consider what the garden is like: beautiful stones, flowers, running streams or simply an undorned and plain field.

3. Move toward the garden as if entering it. Be comfortable in doing so and begin to feel that you now are connected with this place of reflection and prayer.

4. Sit quietly in the garden surrounded by its beauty which reminds one of how it is to be embraced by the presence of God's love. Open your heart to the Presence that draws closer.

5. Begin praying in silence, waiting to listen for guidance. You will know when to speak, questions, or return to silence. Trust your soul for it is ready to hear God's voice.

6. Continue your prayers, both spoken and silent. Perhaps silence will be the greater part, or even all of your prayer time.

7. Leave when prompted by the Holy Spirit to return to your place of daily living. Remember, peacefulness has taken up residence in your life. Live it and give it as you pray your gratefulness to God.

Meet us in our prayers O God, that in these 40 days we might receive your favor of mercy and love as you have given it in Jesus Christ our Lord. Amen.

Easter 1

I heard the echo of wonder
                in that cave
                                destined
for finishing a work
                once begun
                                in the heart of God
'mid mournful sighs
                anguish unrequited
                                saddened souls collapse
worn out hope
                slithers to the ground
                                in pools of grief
while angel blessing
                soothes this darkened prison
                                of binding grave clothes
where Love once tethered
                holds promise with eternity
                                God whispering yes
resounds in heart chambers
                bold triumphs fill hiding places
                                with alleluias
believing dances leap forth
                celebration without bounds
                                vibrations of heavenly joy
I heard the echo of wonder
                in my heart
                                destined for Grace untold
                                Easter 1999

Images for your quiet place

High enough to see other mountains on distant places, Haleakala rises more than 10,000 feet, enabling visitors to see adjoining islands in the Hawaiian chain. Its chilling and strong winds envelop viewers walking the edges or seeking the protection of the look-out shelter. Above sea and city, the clouds have their way, floating easily through the volcanic craters and valleys formed tens of thousands years ago. The oldest stone above sea level is 910,000 years old.

It is a place of wonder where one looks down upon rainbows. There the swift, silent, roiling formations gather the peaks and valleys, as if holding them safely in the arms of Creative genius. Breathing the thin air, moving slowly, you can feel spiritual rising within.

You might like this as a meditation. If so follow these steps:

1. You may have a place that is like this, more familiar to you. You may prefer a quiet valley as opposed to the high mountain. Create the image with your inner eye, one that is the most comfortable.
2. When you have chosen your quiet place, view all that is around you. Scanning slowly, take in every part in a 360 degree circle.
3. Enjoy what you see. Let it be breath-taking. Take your place within all that can be seen. You are part of the landscape as well.
4. Picture the easy, drifting mists flowing before you. It brings healing and soothing coolness to the weary and hurting soul. Let it gently wrap around you as if holding you safely in the arms of Creative Love.
5. Through the gentle softness a rainbow may appear. Perhaps some will look down upon it; others will see it as encircling.
6. Be content to linger as long as you wish. Breathing deeply, allow the mist to recede leaving you in your chosen mountain or valley. Be open to your natural setting.
7. Know that you have been in a Presence that has made itself known. You are guided and protected for your continuing Easter journey.
8. Move slowly into your daily activities. Look for resurrection blessings as the day continues. May the peace you experience be shared with those whom you will meet.

Easter 2

Braided with lacy foam
Surging high and low
Waves carve their presence
Etching contours along
Beaches absorbing pristine matter
Patterned washing from eons
Retrieving ancient sands
Leaving oceanic treasures
Strewn over coastal edges
Where life forms emerge
At borders of Infinity
Rhythmic motions
Swaying souls into One
With life force
Waves of Grace
Tremulous appointed rounds
Receding with age old claims
Immeasurable
Boundless
Everlasting
Scattering deposits of
Rainbow covenants near
Shorelines of wonder
Amending sorrow
Soothing soul grief
Transcending planetary restraint
Resurrection.

Easter, 2002

Images for your quiet place

Easter finery defines the outer edges of our souls as Crocuses and Jonquils define the border of a church lawn. The colorful artistry of Creator pushes through hard crusts of ground and snow covered landscapes announcing the presence and promise of life unforeseen yet soon to be crowned with vitality. Fragrance and color join in transporting the soul as in turning a corner only to behold a startling beauty and we gasp with wonder, breathing all that is surveyed into the soul.

"Landscapes of the Soul" was this year's Lenten theme. Exploring the great spiritual leaders of past and present was underlined with this thought by someone who describes Julian of Norwich and other mystics that "If you live well in your own time, you live well for all times."

As Eastertide, which can be called a soul springtime, begins, consider developing a new landscape within. Try these suggestions as a way of welcoming the resurgence of land and heart and soul:

1. Walking. With weather improving find a pathway for walking and simply enjoy the time, long or short, being where you are.
2. Talking. With a friend you can help one another to find renewal.
3. Looking. With fresh observations notice the ways in which life presents itself. What is new?
4. Seeing. With a time for deeper thought detect metaphors for life.
5. Sharing. With your heart's discernment of God's grace open any new discoveries to your friend.
6. Praying. With your new spiritual environment opening new life say or write your thank you's in whatever way declares the throb of your heart.
7. Acting. With the body and soul refreshed what outcome will take place in what you do with each day? How will this make a difference for you and others? Become a blessing.

Easter 3

Let that ancient cross-like tree
Blossom in my heart
Portal of eternity
Paint with heaven's art
Streams of peace with colors blue
Grace abound with green
In my soul your mercy strew
Forgiving all things mean
Lavender to give joy scent
Reds to make alive
White for One whom heaven sent
Love's great gifts revive
Let rainbows stream from grave's dead-end
Encircle my weary heart
As blossomed branches bow and bend
And sunlight causes clouds to part
O One who mastered wind and wave
Step from cave's dust and grime
Worlds await for you to save
With God's true love sublime
Burst forth O flowers of the field
In yellows of ecstatic wonder
My soul to you this day would yield
In Resurrection hope surrender.

Easter, 2004

Images for your quiet place

How lonely it must have been for the women to arrive at the grave site, and then for Mary to go on alone. How surprising to see the gigantic stone rolled away from the entrance and to find the tomb empty. How amazing to catch the light of day surrounding a familiar silhouette and to hear your name — Mary!

Is this what a quiet morning provides — a way to see with new eyes the very events that once struck you down now raising you up? Is resurrection presented every day before our hearts?

With imagination and your own spiritual tools find your way to an Easter Day with these simple steps to guide you:

1. Picture with your inner eye the the appearance of the grave site where Jesus was placed. Complete the scene by adding hills and rocks and caves of Jerusalem.
2. Gaze at this place where Mary and the disciples sorrowed. Just as your dreams often are stark and drab so it was for them. You may also see this as a place for grieving your lost hopes.
3. Shift your attention to the entrance. Something is so different, so changed from the last time you saw it. Light streams toward you.
4. Feel the warmth of this divine light. Its bright illumination takes form and presence. Hope is restored. Your own dreams return with new energy.
5. Say your name. Listen as it floats before you from a presence you now recognize. Hear your name spoken in a gentle and kind manner.
6. Speak the name of One who is there, "Master!" Let the sound of your voice give you strength and courage, confidence and trust.
7. Leave with a renewed sense of knowing that hopes and dreams, though crushed, still live within just as Christ lives in our world today! Find a way to rejoice and be glad.

May this Easter restore your faith and replenish your service in God's name.

Easter 4

Cold were the stones that lined the dream,
Stilled the sounds of singing birds,
Darkened rays of sunlight beam,
In my heart, my heart.

Garden flowers no longer bright,
Paths no longer spread with joy,
Shadows cast on yearned for light,
In my heart, my heart.

God has listened to this cry,
For my hope had flown away,
Sad my soul did heave a sigh,
In my heart, my heart.

Then with angels in the air,
Rolled the stone that sealed the tomb,
Sorrows lost in loving care,
In my heart, my heart.

Gardens flower as ne'er before,
Pathways gaily show the way,
Love now stands at death's dark door,
In my heart, in my heart

Rise again O Savior dear,
Touch with healing all that dies,
Enter life and be thou near,
In my heart, my heart

                              Easter, 2005

Images for your quiet place

Spring announces Easter when the full moon determines the date. Following this formula Easter falls on the first Sunday following the first full moon following the Vernal Equinox. Easter and the feast of Passover often coincide in the same time of year although this Hebrew feast is celebrated April 23d this year. It is a time for the highest of celebrations. Yearly we are called upon to raise our spirits in jubilation. Life can emerge from the crushing hold of power. Heed the message and free yourself from binding shackles that restrict your life. Follow these steps as a way to find new life:

1. Prepare a place of stillness and comfort. Keep all distraction at a minimum.
2. Breathing deeply fill your lungs inhaling through your nostrils and breathing out with slightly parted lips. If possible for you continue this breathing several times.
3. Imagine with each succeeding breath your body letting go of its tensions and anxieties. You may try watching the tensions leave in some form or symbol as when we exhale in cold weather and "see" our breath; then watch as it disappears.
4. Look carefully at something that restricts, binds or entombs you. Simply look at this part of your life. Let it be outside of you and not a part of you.
5. Become aware of a Love that approaches you and envelops this binding force changing it or casting it away.
6. Feel this wonderful Love embracing you. As it does there comes a welcome that makes you feel at home in the universe.
7. Open your heart and consider who you have now become. The attending power of angelic love has rolled away stones from all that seals you in its cold grasp. Rejoice and be glad for the Divine power of Love.

Easter 5

I know where he is buried
in this twenty-centuries-later-time,
this Good Friday hysteria of ours
challenging postures of war and peace,
calling for the silliness of God's reign;
his goodness nullified as though unpatriotic.

He's been entombed in confusion.
His certainty of Love wrapped up in linen cloths to
keep the stink away,
reminding us of how easily we kill a good thing.
He's in the cold dampness of our confusion
of who is right about what he said and did
and what he means, truly means by God!
He, with his absurd "follow me"
into some maelstrom of certitude
which we have fashioned for ourselves.

But I tell you he will rise! He will rise!
Some day when dawn cracks open this darkness
you will look into emptiness,
hear a voice to not be afraid; he is not here,
and scurry off to tell someone, believing yourself
the news too good to be true.
Then you will see
he meant what he said, what he did, who he was/is
He will no longer be there
where we placed him.
Both of us, all of us, will be free.
An Easter reprise

Easter, 2006

Images for your quiet place

A surprise for the eyes, a surprise for the heart describe Spring and Easter. Slowly the earth is renewing itself. With bells ringing and anthems singing, chancels filled with glorious flowers, and scriptures telling God's love in eloquent voice our souls renew themselves as does the earth. Somehow Easter has helped us to pause and allow another gift that God has handed to us to refresh our souls. Alleluias need not fade in the press of our busy lives and our overstated consumer needs. Turn to a quiet time for yourself. If you are too busy you have even more reason to find solitude, as brief as it may be. Follow these simple steps that offer you peace:

1. Look at your own garden or landscape where you live. If it is warm enough sit outside on a patio or seat near a garden area. Breath in the fresh air. If it is too cool or raining sit by a window.
2. Choose one of your favorite bushes, tree, or plant. Sitting comfortably and away from distractions. Spend a few minutes making your choice. It is all right if you move back and forth, but once you make your choice try to stay with it.
3. Watch as your choice begins to increase in opening its buds. Perhaps a flowering shrub will show color as a Forsythia brings forth a yellow flower.
4. Allow the blossoms to open as in time lapse photos. Enjoy how the delicate revelation brings loveliness and awe to your heart.
5. Observe how other parts of the chosen object change as well. Green leaves may appear, or fruits of some sort. Let this develop without hurry or rushing.
6. Lift your eyes to take in the surrounding area or landscape. See how the part fits into the whole. Enjoy this blending of creation.
7. Use this experience as a special place to which you can return at a moments notice as a surprise for the eyes and your soul and the burial setting of the Easter story.

Easter 6

Thou Creator of Life,
Divider of light and dark,
night and day,
call forth the energy of Love
that death and life combined
would yield new futures,
miracles in the midst of despair,
hope to a wrung out people,
resurrection to darkened spirits.

Thou Creator of Life,
divide the light and dark of our times,
bring forth from sullen graves
glorious energies reclaiming the world,
stir those once chosen
for no one is lost that belongs to you;
startle us so we can see and hear
and rejoice once more.

Thou Creator of Life,
choose any day we pray,
for Love comes when it will
and we have forgotten 'til now;
astonish us with empty tomb
that open the hearts
of our souls,
for the whole universe
trembles because
of Your Infinite Love.

Easter, 2007

Images for your quiet place

Those who ran to the burial place of Jesus, only to run from it, were not prepared for the light which shone forth. The women came to give attention to the remains of a beloved friend only to be startled by a revelation for which few of us are ready. A light coming forth, a voice reassuring, a Presence appearing, must have been overwhelming. We live on this side of the Resurrection. Even though there is a narrative surrounding this event, the coming of Light into our being is awesome. You may prefer to ponder the story and let whatever is there to come forward into your heart or you may choose this way of meditating:

1. Read the Easter story from one of the Gospels by reading it several times or in each of the versions: (Mt. 28:1-10, Mk. 16:1-8, Lk. 24:1-12).
2. Create a garden place, perhaps your own as the burial place in which you find a place to sit down and relax.
3. The surroundings of the Jerusalem grave site are of stone with trees and greenery. Shades of brown rock formations are on either side.
4. After breathing slowly and quieting yourself, simply gaze at what you are seeing. If in your garden, imagine it as a place where the Presence of Jesus is available to you.
5. There is a light which comes forth from the opening to the grave, or in your own corner. It is dim at first but grows in size and brightness.
6. Do not be afraid. You are looking for Jesus of Nazareth . . . an angel voice calls out. The words Fear not! came at Jesus birth, words similar to this time of Resurrection. It is an incredible moment.
7. Looking for Jesus is true of us. Now there may come a special way in which a word is spoken to you, a word one for which you are waiting. "Do not fear" for this is a gift from God.
8. Accept what is happening; God has been looking for us too. It is like home now, a place where we belong. This too is a reality.

9. All you have to do is receive. The day is filled with a strong confidence of not being alone, of prayers being heard, of guidance in the path of life.
10. Give thanks to God, and when ready let the meditation go. Return to your living with the hand of God upon you. Blessings of Easter joy be with you.

Easter 7

Radiance pouring from a shadowed tomb
greeted mourners before Sun could announce the day
and they, once numb, saw with startled eyes
that Death no longer had its way
for somewhere out in heaven's stretch
a greater love had taken place
than what, for some, was power at its best,
though its paltry end was now made useless,
and just as Love, long before, drew from chaos
all the light that was needed,
so these simple and innocent hearts
had in sweet earnest come,
catching the grin of Almighty
who surprised and healed their aching souls,
naming in gentle voice and love
one who had come in heartache's duty
and still speaks today,
your name and mine,
beside rolled-away stones of entombed events
bringing God's Easter enterprise
anytime, anywhere, today,
and thus
Springtime to your heart.

Easter, 2008

Images for your quiet place

Little did the women know that the morning would hold such a greeting. What began as a traditional aspect of caring for the dead suddenly and alarmingly became a leap in astonished believing. Out of divine light, a spectacular illumination, their world changed and so did ours. The sound of names being spoken by a familiar voice was almost too much. A credible question is "what is happening?" Even for us it is a question not of the past but of our own time. When Easter comes and resurrection themes are spoken and sung, it is our experience, our beholding, our wonder taking place. Still the question stays with us, "what is happening?"

Pondering the thought of Easter holds some answers for us but what of deeper stirrings of the heart, the knowing of resurrection without being able to give it any logic?

Consciousness today opens a mysterious wonder which leaves the beholder in awe. If the connection we have is only a small cave for burial, then much is lost. The brightness of the first Easter waits in the scriptures.
1. Turn to any of the Gospels, perhaps all three of the stories. Read the account aloud do that your voice is an instrument through which the words are heard.
2. Reread the special passage that stands out for you. Keep reading the words over and over until you are content to offer full attention to one outstanding thought.
3. Let this inmost idea be the illumination that comes forth from an empty tomb which itself cannot contain the light of God.
4. You may hear your name, or that of someone else. Perhaps a word of guidance and hope will come to you or a direction that is most needed.
5. Easter offers new life and hope. Gladly receive it as the gift from the generous Giver of Love. God blesses you in these quiet Easter moments.

Pentecost 1

Pentecost celebrates the giving of the Torah to Moses on Mt. Sinai; for the early Christian community Pentecost celebrates the giving of the Holy Spirit. Thunder, lightening and thick clouds on a mountain top in Exodus and the "rush of a violent wind . . . Divided tongues, as of fire" in Acts are the descriptions of scripture for magnificent presence of God's powerful work in human experience. Please read Exodus 19:11-25 and Acts 2: 1-4 or as much as you wish. Please accept the following words from my meditation on these two Biblical narratives.

No wind is ill that blows such good
  cross soul prairies
  in pioneer days spent surveying
  spiritual landscapes wished to be known
Sweeping with desert heat and mountain cold
  Life breath into breathing
  igniting embers from past fires of passion
  once energized by heart-filled embraces
  smoldering from weary neglect
  and imposed realities thought to be truth
Smoke ascends from dutiful prayers
  brushing the sky while Spirit rushes
  languages from everywhere whisper
  cosmic secrets from the Heart of Being
  flames snap their command to listen
Chambers of Creation have much to say
  observing Love greater than earth power
  broken tablets-broken hearts mended
  see as Creator sees
  love as Creator loves
Live now in this world with vigorous Hope
  for no wind is ill that blows such good.
          Pentecost, 1997

Images for your quiet place

An old Television program, *You Are There,* created an historical event and placed you within its context, staging an exact replica of a particular time. These images are much like that except their purpose is to provide a meditation or prayer-like state in which you can experience the deepest of meanings of a recorded biblical time. The season of Pentecost is one of ecstatic celebration. *Images* issues an invitation to return to one of the oldest times in Christian history, sometimes called the birthday of the Church. Follow this simple formula as a meditative tool for your silent praying:

1. Find a dictionary of the Bible and look up Pentecost. Let this description help you develop the staging for the event.

2. Sit quietly while the scenery unfolds before you. Both the dictionary and the Bible record will help you visualize the scene.

3. Move slowly into the picture you have created. There were some 3,000 persons at this special time when Peter and the disciples spoke of Jesus. If you know Peter's sermon repeat it to yourself. You may also read it.
    Of course you can always keep your distance viewing what is taking place as if in a theater.

4. Listen to the words, the excitement of the crowd, that accusation about being drunk and Peter's apologetic about the resurrection.

5. Imagine hearing several languages in the crowd's response. There is something about how they are responding that helps you understand beyond the language barrier.

6. Observe the surge of those who seek to be baptized. Watch as they move toward the river and are gently received into the gathering community soon to be recognized as followers of the way.

7. Take your leave of this time of meditative prayer, returning to your daily life with renewed energy. Pray your thankfulness to God.

Pentecost 2

Angels carry us
        to purging flames
                from the Anywhere
that is our home
        with swift winds
                lifting their wings
to the Everywhere
        home of Creative Love
                rushing delirious ecstasy
spinning excited souls
        languages pouring forth
                in ultimate tongues of praise
singing as never before
        let loose in abundant joy
                flowering heart meadows
fragrancing the air
        deluding wine accusations
                favoring exuberant dance
older than earth-angels
        showering gifts of power
                and sweet welcoming vitality
in unsuspecting gatherings
        waiting for all that is new
                for angels carry us far
to spatial heavens of birth
        finding where our breath has come
                and where it shall return
in the house of Providence
        forever.

                Pentecost, 1999

Images for your quiet place

The harvest festival was taking place; fields were filled with bounteous beauty. The hand of God was evident in the glorious display of wheat with its waving, dancing joy, looking as if strings were being strummed by a master musician, sending music that can only be detected by the listening heart. The day was Pentecost; awareness was at its highest. Ordinary experiences collapsed under the weight of exuberant outpourings of the Holy Spirit. Be open to the Divine Consciousness that willingly pours itself into mind and heart. These steps may be followed:

1. Develop a picture of a blowing wheat field with your inner eye. Through its waving grain you are beckoned to enter. When ready to accept the invitation, do so stepping easily and quietly, allowing the entire field to envelop and embrace.
2. Give yourself time to look around and enjoy the field just for its sheer beauty and wonder.
3. Begin a slow walk; no hurry is necessary in this realm. All will come easily as you come into this space of creative love
4. Move deeply through the rows of golden joy; feel wrapped in a new awareness of the Divine filling you with presence and healing.
5. Touch the soul where heavenly inspiration begins its peaceful entry into your heart. Allow this to happen in a slow, light manner. There is no rushing here, no time table, no deadline. There is no time, other than the celestial working that has its own order. There is no harm, only healing, calming, opening.
6. Breathe deeply to attune yourself to the hum of the Universe. (When we are in our quietest moments we vibrate in the same cycle as the earth.)
7. Pause briefly and listen to what is spoken or sung. Open your heart and listen.
8. Walk once more; complete the circle through the field and return to its edge, looking where you have been; say a prayer of thankfulness for all you have experienced.
9. Return to the life into which you have been born. Now you have found how wide and deep the generosity is from the Creator. Pray in the way that you have found to be best, thanking God for the gifts given to your heart and mind.
10. Live the new life. Enjoy and embrace it!

Pentecost 3

If you listen carefully
you may hear a multitude
speaking
in languages not known
but easily understood
there in your heart
where fire has its birth
and wind takes you beyond time
if you listen carefully
and have no need except
a gentle flowing brook
transporting your soul
not touching earth
only shores of heaven
if you listen carefully
you will hear more
than ever dreamed
bursting seams of language
surrounding
whirling deep within
touching
warming
healing with
flaming fervor
ardent desires
soul consuming
passions
if you listen carefully.

Pentecost, 2001

Images for your quiet place

In the story of Pentecost, (known in Hebrew celebrations as Shavuoth or Festival of Weeks) four elements are present: earth, water, fire, air. Earth is present in the agricultural feast when two loaves of bread, baked from the new crop of wheat, were brought by Jewish families to the Temple as an offering. Bread was broken at this early Christian festival. Fire was present in the hearts of those gathered; water was used in the baptism of three thousand people, and the rushing wind of the Holy Spirit was upon them. (Read the story in Acts 2.)

Using the elements develop a ritual of quiet, personal meditation. You will need: bread symbolizing the earth, water in a bowl or a natural body of water, fire which may be simply a candle, and for wind an open window with an in-coming breeze, the outdoors, or a small fan. Take each element on separate days or all at once prayerfully and thankfully.

1. Bake or buy fresh bread. If it is freshly baked feel its warmth in your hands. Place your warmed hands over your heart for a few minutes. Then pray these words or your own: To You Creator of the Universe, from whose great earth this bread has come, warm my soul and nourish my body to live for you. Amen. Then remain in a silence.

2. Whatever your source of water, (flowing water over rocks, or a living body of water), listen to sound emanating from it. When ready, dip your fingers or hand into the water and gently move it to your head that it flows over you. Pray this or your own words: Creator of the Universe, who fills the water with life, renew my body and soul in this immersion of your holy water. Amen.

3. Fire glowing in a fireplace, on a candlestick or an outdoor fireplace symbolizes the great power inherent in flames. Watch its excited dancing, its sway with the wind, its crackle from the embedded earth elements. Safely draw near and simply gaze, focusing on the flames. Light and heat enters within. Pray as you wish or with this prayer: Creator of the Universe, whose passion is like the fire before me, consume my heart and soul and body with your desire of love that we may be one. Amen.

4. Now the source of wind that is available comes upon you. It wraps itself around your body, fluffs your hair, enters your nostrils, changes your body temperature. Pray this if you wish: Creator of the Universe, wind and breath of my life, stir deeply my soul, and join my spirit with your Spirit, wind upon my body, heart held by love, Amen.

Pentecost 4

Fire
is best left in the heart
bale-fire
consuming
purging
forgiving
extending prayer hands
crackling praise to heaven
wisps of smoke
souls really saying something
for a change
after tons of word ashes
feeling passionate
erotic
full bodied
lunging toward destiny
made for this
primal callings
charged with life
as lovers mesh
white with heat
bonfires of ecstasy
consummations of spirit
with Spirit.

Pentecost, 2002

Images for your quiet place

In a conversation with Nicodemus, Jesus speaks of being born again, of renewal, likening rebirth to a wind which comes upon you. "What is born of flesh is flesh, and what is born of Spirit is spirit. Do not be astonished that I said to you, 'You must be born from above.' The wind blows where it chooses, and you hear the sound of it, but you do not know where it comes from or where it goes. So it is of everyone who is born of the Spirit. (John 3.)

Wind, often identified as God, tugs and pushes. While standing on a hill the blustery current can have its way with us. It whistles through towns and streets with merry tunes while dancing and hopping in dusty minuets. Squalls pinch cheeks and demand us to turn up our coat collars. We lean into the wind as swirling gusts encircle us with its will. Then in some mysterious way it becomes a breeze that caresses us; a balm to aid in soothing and healing our skin and our souls.

Follow these suggestions as you meditate; bring utmost attention to the wind.

1. Find a comfortable place where you can sit or stand alone. With the purpose of being caught by the wind, and finding renewal or rebirth, look closely at your surroundings, your chosen place.

2. Record in your journal the day, time, temperature, and place. Count the ways in which you can see the presence of wind: trees moving, tall grasses swaying, lawns rustling, flowers bending and turning back to the sun's gracious light.

3. Close your eyes. Feel the wind which takes its own form and knows how to approach you. Open yourself, your nostrils, your whole being, breathing in freshness of spirit.

4. With your inner eye picture yourself as a tree being strengthened by its blustery but friendly manners. So the Spirit makes strong the major elements of your life, your soul.

5. Move to a scene of tall grasses which resemble our yearning wishes, and observe new patterns as if a hand is in the middle designing a unique pattern of beauty.

6. Flowers and grass are now being massaged as if by a silent hand. They face the light which draws forth glorious color and joyful presence which can be our daily life.

7. Now remain in this quiet given to you. What you see in the trees, grasses and flowers is like the Spirit that moves within you, restoring—born again—as if a Pentecost for your soul.

Pentecost 5

What fire has ever burned
That did not also torch my heart
And bring to ashes
Simmering old intentions
Of grandiose spiritual triumphs
Of my own

What wind did ever blow
Catching embers of a dream
Creating a blaze of truth
Ignited with love
From beyond my heart

What language sound
Erupting amid babble
In eloquent ecstacy
Would say more than any words
Singing out my soul's speech

How could I be so captured
By earth-bound feelings
Knowing love as lovers know
All sense in jubilant dance
Heaven and earth in symphonic harmony

Sweep me in your arms
Great Love
And tell me of your wish
For I your servant will be
In festivals of fiery joy.

Pentecost, 2003

Images for your quiet place

Prepare for this imagery by reading Acts 2.

In the season of Pentecost the liturgical color is red. It describes visually the great celebration and consuming fire dancing upon disciples' heads and within their hearts. Pentecost tells of the power of the wind which moved amid a space crowded by several nations of people. The sweeping movement of the Holy Spirit was upon the entire assembly and yet was beyond any language. Pentecost is not confined to an historical time, although it is the birthday of the Church. Such an experience can be appreciated in your own life. It is one way this can take place for you.

1. Take a few minutes to visualize a garden of splendor. The wind moves the surroundings; trees and flowers sway at its command.

2. See yourself as standing, or sitting, or walking through this garden place. It may be more comfortable to look upon it from afar.

3. Allow the colors of red and green to stand out. These complimentary colors bring vitality (red) and calm (green).

4. Surround yourself in this garden with red Carnations, and their green stems. Add Nasturtiums, Impatiens, salvias, and ruby chard.

5. Look upon the vibrant reds as if they are flames coming down as the Holy Spirit resting upon heart and mind.

6. Sit quietly as this image touches as if a wind is blowing through your life. Be ready and open for the many surprises of God's energizing actions.

7. Make use of God's gift to you in some new enterprise of charity and hope. Let yourself be sent forth with a message of compassion for all.

Pentecost 6

Ignite my soul O Love Divine
Set fire to my heart
Touch the tinder from my tears
Like shavings on a hearth
Blaze with fury all my fears
Come in with rushing wind
Glow with dance in my heartbeat
Let love with awe now blend
Sear with passion's loving heat
Ecstatic joy now send
Forge throughout this soul forlorn
Where once my soul did weep
Love for me that you have borne
So wondrous and so deep
Language is without a word
Perhaps my soul shall leap
Ardent gifts of Spirit flash
And dance upon my head
Other visions turned to ash
When I am with Thee wed
Take this self and make anew
My vow to love Thee best
Make my fondest dream come true
Thy love shall be my rest.

Pentecost, 2004

Images for your quiet place

" . . . it was impossible for him (Jesus) to be held by its power (death)" (Acts 2:24). Peter's sermon on the occasion of Pentecost refers to the Omnipotence of God as witnessed in Jesus Christ. Here the resurrection is assured as the Holy Spirit rushes into human life in the form of a mighty wind to declare that the impossible took place, that death has no stronghold over life, no power by which love can be dimished or defeated.

Tongues of fire, rushing winds, words beyond ordinary speech; how forceful the entrance of the Holy Spirit upon this gathering of devoted women and men, followers of Jesus. Peter is proclaiming God's power which makes all things possible. In our own devotion we can find a way to be open to the power which the Holy Spirit bestows upon us.

Do the following:
1. Read the story of Pentecost in the second chapter of Acts. Continue to read it several times, slowly and with devotion.

2. Imagine yourself as being part of the Pentecost gathering. Peter is addressing the crowd; some are followers of Jesus and others bystanders.

3. Notice those around you. They come from many nations clothed in a way which indicates their origin. Look at how they are alike and how they are different.

4. Listen to their speech. Responding with excitement to Peter's words, each one tells the Jesus story in their own way, their own words, their own language.

5. Feel the power of the Holy Spirit being unleashed. It has the force of wind, the heat of fire, the excitement of a marvelous discovery.

6. Open your heart in an act of receiving. As a participant in the story, it becomes your own festival, celebrating your personal dedication as a follower.

7. Give action to being a disciple of Christ to make the impossible come true.

Pentecost 7

This fire you kindle in my soul
like none I've known before,
Whence came its power to make me whole,
desiring, wanting more?

Into my chambered heart you sweep
with kind and gentle word,
so warm and sweet my heart doth weep
with tears I ill afford.

How does this burning now declare
the deepest love I know
I must not yield; I must forbear,
yet tremble not to go.

You grasp me in your passion fierce,
no breathe is left in me,
heart's deepest cold your love does pierce;
old life shall never be.

Great Lover, here's my body, soul
for you have set me free
to fly with joy o'er every knoll;
the mountains and the sea.

Is that a star you made for me
that's shining high and bright?
that says our love shall ever be
with soft and tender might.

And thus your Holy Spirit came
A Pentecost ago
My living, loving ne'er the same
My heart for you aglow.

Pentecost, 2006

Images for your quiet place

Calendars pinpoint particular events. These accent our celebrations, in community and personally. In following the church year, the repetition of special days gives a focus to the heart and mind. Yet, these same occasions have the power to burst upon you at any time. The feeling of a joyful Christmas takes you by surprise on a hot July day. Easter suddenly surrounds you with hope as you walk through a garden. Pentecost with its power symbolized by fire, languages melting in to one single moment of praise, and personal excitement about the Presence of the Holy Spirit, are not confined to either history or a single, historic date.

In order to bring a Pentecost experience please use this style of Lectio Divina:

1. Seek a quiet place that is largely undisturbed by ordinary noise. Free yourself from telephones, cell phones, and traffic.

2. Find a comfortable position for yourself, sitting with a straight, but not strained posture.

3. Read the Pentecost story in Acts 2: 1-12. Continue to read this story until a verse, a phrase, or a single word stands out for you.

4. Give your full attention to whatever may come from your reading. Regard this as a gift from God to you through the scriptures.

5. Spend as much time as needed to entertain this focus in both mind and heart.

6. Pray your thankfulness for this special gift as you converse with God. Be open to this conversation, praying and listening until your soul has emptied itself.

7. Dwell with God in quietness and peace by letting go of all thought and distraction and enjoy the deepest sense of Presence as it comes upon you with its healing power. Feel whole again.

About Calendar Seasons

Our daily lives give opportunities for celebration and happiness through calendar days as well as the liturgical year. Friends, families, and communities are restored in special events, i.e. birthdays, anniversaries, homecomings, vacations, memorials and national recognitions. Changing seasons and national holidays are all interwoven in our life.

To give these days recognition, summer, autumn, and thanksgiving are added to the liturgical days in the hope that they will remind you of good times, even those that may have been tense, and of festivities that renew your spirit. Each of them is designed to prompt your writing and remembering thoughts of your personal experience. Here you may create your own images that will guide you into a realm of peacefulness beyond the day itself. May you find healing and hilarity as you open your mind and heart.

Summer 1

Sweet sounds
open mornings as delicate
wrens chortle happiness over nesting
warmth, moving summer on to its next
adventure. Singing in the midst of storms,
undaunting spirits announce better things to
come. Welcome all who breathe and toast the
day with hopping presences and gathering of winter
stores for summer is short and there is much yet to be
done. The earth is good; generous is its supply for all.
What more could we have ever asked when needs have
been met before our asking; wisdom providing, long
before desire arose, or hungers reminding, or even
thoughts understanding? Little wonder such joyful
laughing entertains our souls, for God's language
is spoken in such mirth and celebration;
worship it is, and we would do well
if our mornings opened thus, with
shout and glee and hope to meet
and conquer all adversity.
1996

Summer 2

Soft, delicate clouds pass over head
crossing back-scratching mountain tops
thick and foamy, thin and wispy
bearings charted by One who made them.

What collections of pain and misery,
of sorrow and anguish, leaping hope
and laughing memories do you carry
from places once visited and passed over?

Do you carry the prayers rising from
smoldering ruins, broken hearts, the
fire of destruction in Kosovo and
too many other cities to name?

Carry then this prayer too from
the heart which leaps at your beauty
rain balm upon the destitute and forsaken
chilled souls in little Colorado towns.

Tell them that hope is on the way
in the home of the brave, land of the free
tell them daring souls are not all gone
write in clear skies charters of human kindness.

Drift over oceans wide and turbulent seas
bless every land on which your shadow falls
that eyes cast down may look up once again
and see, really see, that life is holding forth.

The One who gives your bearing o'er this earth
gives to us this charted way we often miss
make pure and clean each soul's desire
as drifting clouds with quiet hope-filled dreams.
1999

Summer 3

Summer my life with glorious blue
Divine assortments of celestial hue
Restore my being with elegant pleasure.

Summer my body with sunlit rays
Set my flesh in passionate blaze
Wrap me up in a tropical breeze
Caress me tight with a cherub's squeeze.

Summer my mind with undersea brilliance
Prompt sweet desires of heated dalliance
As Seagulls in the distance float
Fly me to notions of secret hope.

Summer my soul as a lover wild
Enchanting moments of love adore
My own return to Eden once more.
(from the sands of Redington Beach, Florida)
2004

Summer 4

Angel wings brushed across the sky
when divided night and day coverged,
before breath was given
or life emerged,
dripping from its watery past.

Playgrounds of color grew
as swirling chaos backed down,
all that was and yet to be
found place in wombs of calm
eager to shrug all days before.

What drew you from that soggy berth
springing forth in beauteous praise?
Did singing bird call you forth,
your soul in glory, then to raise
in awe and find your breath?

Would my eyes reflect such hues
as first you brushed the sky?!
Is it I who then did first arise
or only now did gasp; is it I
in whom creation writes of love?

O that my soul be like that sky
on which love's color is writ,
no speech or words is yet to be
for heart and mind remit
as when first breath inhaled.
sunset somewhere on Plum Lake, Saynor, WI
2008

Autumn 1

Soft descending of summer green
              whirling updrafts sudden shower
                         settle in drifting hues
leafy remnants in seasonal brown
              lay in paths quickly changing
                         as if by Spirit's choosing
mysterious footsteps pushing ahead
              foliage now crisp and brittle
                         scurrying for safety
proceed to hiding places from wintry oaths
              clinging piles in one last chance
                         to find secluded havens
as with my soul memories falling
              caught in spontaneous swirls
                         of Holy prompting
Divine steps uncovering footwalks
              where none were seen before
                         clearing old matters away
heaping drudgery aside
              reclaiming earth destinies
                         in huddled moments of hope
suddenly spinning their whirlpools
              resettling strength and courage
                         for blasts of pending cold
once so fragile now yielding
              broken for Creation's larger intent
                         sacrament of service
celestial schemes inviting
              willing hearts committed into
                         Holy Hands of Love
for resurrection spring
              promises in leafy descents
                         circle of lovely care
compassionate beckoning
              of my soul replenished by grace
                         returning and returning
ever to live as Love as loved.

Autumn 2

Tinted leaves in soft descent
                    Lay multi-colored blankets of beauty
along well traveled paths
              creating passages transformed into walkways
with heralding announcements of Presence
                  crisp and dry leaves crackle in fullness
of joy
        cycles of pleasure from beyond
                    showing forth an ancient path of life
in whatever trail was chosen
              eternal esplanades with shores of wonder
seasons of renewal
          crisscrossing sad flower strewn processions
a slow march
       bereavement for love's brief tokens given
                      disease ridden
anguished and abandoned
             unheard of places being heard
                     listening hearts
right hands filled with pleasures meek and mild
                  bestowing soft touches
forgotten souls on a path of life
              You choose whom you wish for Love
misery's courtyard of majestic service
                crown those who hear—see
tear stained paths wait for such seasons
          where souls empty out their precious life
until the day is gone
         and all paths poor and rich turn heavenward
Pleasure's Kingdom for all.

    May God bless and rest the souls of Princess Diana and Mother
Teresa who showed the path of life and charity.
              1997

Autumn 3

Drift sweetly through the air
    mother trees sigh to falling leaves
gently place your head upon the earth
    summer burdens now complete
restful journeys wait
    collecting winds transporting
once green now brown orange red yellow
    brittle
dancers waving winging
    greeting next world enterprise
huddling and bunching
    like soul and self
under deepening blue of sky
    seeing beyond *beyond*
creation in soothing lullabies
    closing days and years
rest *rest* quietly now
    seasons of fruitfulness passing
yields of sumptuous banqueting
    plenteous sharing of earth
summer burdens now complete
    soul work closing *closing*
full cycle revelations
    scraping scooping holding promises
primal eden waiting
    presences in peaceful company
one with One *One*
    earliest first breaths
now beginning in earthy surround
    rising from dust and ash
Divine and human entwined by Love
    as it was . . . . so it is . . . . shall be
2000

Autumn 4

Kicking dry and fragile leaves
Crisp green edged browns
Dried from lows of cooler air
Sailing briefly in a swirl
Circling around in patterns
Invisible in ordinary walking
Pathways easily followed
Now more clearly seen
As rhythmic life
Also crisp and edged with green
Weaves its single way
Into depths of the Universe
As soul journeys turn
Close and far
Around unknown centers
Containing deeper passions
Igniting soul ventures yet to be
Calling
Beckoning the heart
Transforming magic
For waiting worlds
With ordinary avenues
Where kicking leaves
Display patterns yet to be
Labyrinth of ancient days
Sacred pathway of love
Birthing wonder of hope.
2002
(From an inspired moment walking the Labyrinth at Weber Center,
Adrian, Michigan. Dr. Lauren Artess, Facilitator)

———

Autumn 5

Skies blemished with missile trails
Pocked and broken earth deserts
Humans kneel in pleading wails
Invade our troubled lands
Angel armies
Such a prayer prevails
In silence
Above screaming sirens
And nightly army fired
Angel troops and regiments
Give flesh to mercy
In stone cold hearts
Sculp images of compassion
From each nation-soul inspired
Pull from wells of deep desires
Waters that heal
Draw that all may drink
Elixirs of Eden wonders
United as long ago
Companions in Creator walks
In earthly gardens of hope
Oh angels armed with love
Send shock and awe
As it is above.

(This poem was written for the International Society of Poets Convention and Symposium in Washington, D.C. August 15—17, 2003. It was added to the World's Largest Poem for Peace in the world.)

Autumn 6

Waiting
>On a near frosty, crisp and blue October day
>for trees to free their leaves,
>for their chlorophyll factories to shut down
>letting loose the annual barrage of hidden colors.

Waiting
>for their decorating patterns to cover my path
>for me to see when my head is bending low;
>rainbows, reminding me that God has not forgotten
>how many times I only see forbidding gray.

Waiting
>for sunlight to betray ominous threats of storm
>to a world as small as mine;
>as if to end it abruptly without fanfare
>and so mark a shriveled soul's demise.

Waiting
>for someone to take note that I really know,
>all along my soul knows better than that;
>and makes of my bending low a prayer,
>reading rainbow leaves of good fortune.

Waiting
>for bare and darkened limbs to stand in stately praise,
>stretching upward to scratch open skies of abundance
>and pour blessings upon my fretting soul,
>soothing my fevered dreams.

Waiting
>for a quiet winter day filled with graceful snow
>inviting new patterns to make the covered way
>returning me to my ever repeated
>and welcomed resurrection.

2006

Thanksgiving 1

I thank you,
      Thou Heart of the Universe
for all the gifts which have made up my life:
      for sunrise announcing the faithful encircling of Love,
      for the morning air which refreshes body and soul,
      for the greeting of bird-songs reflecting the first sound,
      for the energy of walking and moving as the dance of life,
      for the gradual populating of my space so I am not alone,
      for the blessings of work asking my mind and heart to play,
      for the noonday sun heating the day as the fire of passion,
      for the joining of common interest to give great cause,
      for the dusk bringing coolness as compassionate healing,
      for the dark of night breathing relief from all troubles,
      for the dutiful round which soothes my bruises giving life,
I thank You,
      Thou Heart of the Universe
      for all the gifts which make up my life.

      Bless the Lord, my soul;
          my innermost heart, bless his holy name.
      Bless the Lord, my soul,
          and forget none of his benefits.
      Psalm 103;1,2 (NEB)
          1996

Thanksgiving 2

I pause to say thanks to my Creator
  and I saw the sky in a different way
  with velvet hues of gold and pink
  it stopped me short and made me think
the promise is true—it is a new day.

I paused to say thanks to my Creator
  and I saw the tress in a different way
  long branches now bare for winter's rest
  buds forming—awaiting Spring's test
the promise is true—it is a new day.

I paused to say thanks to my Creator
  and I saw the earth in a different way
  its yield of bounty and plentiful food
  reveling in creation's word "It is good"
the promise is true—it is a new day.

I paused to say thanks to my Creator
  and I saw those around me in a different way
  the same as I—hunger, cold and shabby bare
  I have the bounty, the plenty and love to share
the promise is true—it is a new day.

            1992

Thanksgiving 3

May thankfulness
> like solar flares burst over my heart
> and search therein each crevice
> where hidden lies untouched romance
> that sings of unfolding passion
> uncontained and unrestrained
> mighty with unfettered endowments
> until with blaze equal to the Sun
> searches out shadowed lives
> kept secret under bridge bellies
> curled over sidewalk grates
> shivering in cardboard tenements
> park bench solitudes with
> safe deposit shopping carts

May thankfulness
> ignite with celestial compassion
> compelling hands to extend
> feet to walk
> eyes to see and ears to hear
> hearts to find new hearts
> vibrating with universal hum
> one with one with One

May thankfulness
> stretch my soul.
> 1999

Thanksgiving 4

I bow my head as thankfulness floods my heart

> for Light of God which fills the Universe
> > and causes chaos to tremble
> for undaunted soul of America
> for spirit of unity binding all who love freedom
> for perseverance in the search for life
> for tears which fill each eye for someone lost
> for tears which fill each eye for someone found
> for prayers ascending with dust and smoke
> for untiring dedication on top of rubble
> for unknown acts of heroism
> for bravery in common folk
> for hidden sacrifice for another
> for nations still able to grieve deep wounds
> for chills when singing America the Beautiful
> for never ending hope pervading evil
> for freedom unafraid to give voice to dissent
> for Truth prevailing over presumed truths
> for liberty which spreads justice for all
> for final triumph of soul when life is close

I bow my head as thankfulness floods my heart.

(Written in tribute for victims and families of 9-11-01)

Thanksgiving 5

Seeing first Sun rising
Hearing first bird singing
Tasting first fruit growing
Feeling first breeze flowing
Smelling first fragrance wafting

Sun opening dawn
Bird singing love
Fruit sweetening pleasure
Breeze caressing flesh
Fragrance telling presence

Bountiful gift
Unspeakable joy
Sensual delight
Daily companion
Spirit rejoicing

Generous giving
Humble accepting
Life renewing
Love returning
Thankful praising
2002

Thanksgiving 6

Thank you for all that I can see
Your wonders that shall always be
For light that shines beyond each cloud
For stars that light a traveler proud
And when my eyes no longer view
My inner sight reveals You.

Thank you for all that I can hear
For distant trains and laughter near
For children singing in sweet voice
For old folks, babies with their choice
And when my ears no longer catch
My soul Your whispers then would match.

Thank you for all that I can taste
Our table by Your love is graced
For plum puddings and cherry pie
For loving hands through meals doth fly
When I can no longer savor
Sweet water flows from our savior.

Thank you for all that I can smell
My body's gift doth serve me well
For times when fragrance calms my soul
For breeze filled scents that make me whole
And when I can no longer trace
My mind recalls each flower filled vase.

Thank you for all that I can feel
Your vibrant love that makes me heal
For softer skins that give delight
For warm embrace that brings Your light
And when I can no longer touch
My soul Your Presence then doth vouch.
                    2006

Thanksgiving 7

I place before thee my thankful heart
        for memories which lie undisturbed
        untouched by the wiles of men and nature
            resting in a pleasant garden
            adorned with peacefulness
            flowered by these gifts of love:

        friendships that endure through pain and suffering,
        understanding when I cannot explain,
        sustaining grace when I go awry,
        support when I am weak,
        acceptance when I find it hard to accept myself,
        encouragement when my dreams fade,
        healing embraces when my heart is heavy,
        kind words when my day is harsh,
        inspiring worship that opens my soul,
        charity that warms my being,
        Presence when I am alone,
        above all, family warmth when all else is cold.

I place before thee my thankful heart
        as I take notice of love surrounding me,
         a treasured gift of God.
           2005

Thanksgiving 8

For this I give my thanks, O God
playful squirels that climb my trees
dogs chasing smells on a breeze
birds that flit through branches high
soaring eagles in the sky
puppies that chew upon my boot
owls that just don't give a hoot
little kids with backpacks filled
helping friend when all is spilled
winter's cold and runny nose
chilling ice that freezes toes
harvest days when crops come in
hints of change the winds blow in
each day I see Creation's best
leaves that fall and trees at rest
dried up plants all turning brown
snow falls snuggling on earth's crown
bayberry candles subtle scent
flames that flicker with content
shadowed pilgrims once so brave
spreads of goodness that God gave
corn stalks on the worn out fields
scarecrows watching yearly yields
tables set with welcome cheer
with God's presence drawing near.
For this I give my thanks, O God
2008

A Reflection from the author

It is the hope and prayer of the author that here you find references upon which to design spiritual pathways that are fulfilling and inspiring. To that end the poetry and guided images were gathered from many years of pastoral experiences, meditation, and keeping journals.

To provide these writings became a mission of my wife, Elsie, and I for those who are interested in a journey of the heart and soul. With the encouragement of family and friends and those who asked for spiritual guidance, this book became a reality. Its purpose is to lead the reader to a new beginning. There is no closing of this manual to guide your spiritual pathway, rather it is like a welcoming door that stands open at all times. You have taken steps toward a pilgrimage. Now this journey becomes your spiritual pathway. Continue on with our blessings.

CPSIA information can be obtained
at www.ICGtesting.com
Printed in the USA
FFHW02n0819251018
48980369-53227FF